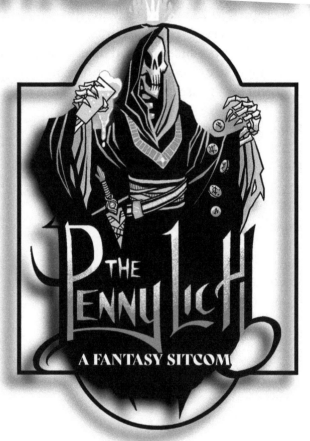

THE PENNY LICH
A FANTASY SITCOM

Volume 2

Printed in the United States of America

First Printing, 2022

ISBN Ebook - 978-1-7364618-5-3
Paperback - 978-1-7364618-4-6

The Odd Empire
675 NW 2nd Ave
Canby, OR, 97013

www.TWClawson.com

Front cover art by:
Adam Scythe
@adamscythe_art

Penny Lich Logo designed by:
Barbara Guttman
www.marteani.art

These three stories are dedicated to three friends;

Brianna Fenty
Devani Anjali
Paul Davis

This would have never happend without you three.
This is all your fault.

T.W. CLAWSON

THE PENNY LICH

A FANTASY SITCOM

Cleric without a God

The Penny Lich is empty, quiet, serene. Particles of dust dance in the streams of light that jet forth from the frosted windows. Wooden pillars helping hold the second floor up cut the light and give off the scent of rustic comfort. The leather chairs in front of the fireplace sit cold, no flame to warm them up. Candles hold still, waiting in anticipation for the spark of life to come to them.

A drink sits on the bar, a solitary and half-filled beer. Its amber colors catch the light and reflect off its condensation into the world around it. Filling and satisfying breath forces its way into Hadvar's lungs. His peppered beard filters the air through his nose and moves out of the way as he exhales. The Tavern, Hadvar's domain, is peaceful. No matter how many hands it has been exchanged into, it has always been his. It's times like this that he's reminded of a life worth living, peaceful and content.

The door to the tavern opens and the happy moment in the Penny Lich is gone.

"Hurry, get him up on the table!" Elliot shouts. A crowd of people rush in and a roar of pain trails in on the shoulders of Sycilia and Moses. An improvised stretcher carries Aarik as he writhes in agony.

Hadvar sets his drink down, exhales, and says a soft prayer.

"Hadvar!" Elliot shouts as he points Moses and Sycilia to a table. Several glasses get knocked over and a candle flies. Gwen comes in with Ella and Brohn. "Hadvar, I need a bottle of something strong!"

"Whisky? Rum?"

"How about an old fashioned?" Brohn says, sitting at the bar.

"Brohn." Gwen slaps him. "Don't be a dick. He needs it for the wound."

Aarik lays on the table, Sycilia holding him down. "Where's it at, bro? Where's it at!?"

"It's running up, aaaaaah!" Aarik yells as he goes for his leg. "Ah! My leg!"

"Don't touch it!" Moses commands. "I'm trying to heal the damage as it cuts through. Elliot, I need you to hurry!"

"Booze!" Elliot shouts. "Now!"

Hadvar grabs the first bottle he can get his hands on. "Here!"

"No!" Brohn shouts. The party looks over at him, concern flowing from his eyes. "Sorry, that's King's Casket Whiskey..."

"So?" Elliot says, annoyed.

"It's just a really expensive and rare bottle," Brohn says, unnerved. Elliot looks back to Hadvar, who just gives an affirmative shrug.

"It doesn't matter." Elliot takes the bottle and bites the cork off. "His life is worth more than a bottle of whiskey." Standing over Aarik, Elliot can see the penetration mark on Aarik's leg. "Here we go, we got you the good stuff, bud."

Aarik's neck strains in absolute torture, face is covered in tears and misery. His eyes shoot open after noticing Elliot standing over him with the bottle.

"NO! Hey, whoa! No, Elliot!" Aarik screams.

"I know, it'll hurt, but we need to clean the wound, and get this thing out of you."

"No, I know, but you can't use that. It's the best bottle of whisky I've ever had!"

"What?" Elliot looks exhausted.

"Aarik, come on," Sycilia says. "There is a moore worm burrowing inside of you, and you wanna save some booze?"

"Sycilia, you have no idea," Aarik says in pain. "Brohn and I had a glass of it and now we're best friends. It's that good."

"You're best friends?" Moses asks, a little offended.

"Hey," Elliot snaps.

"Yeah," Brohn says. "The other day, we were just hanging out and Hadvar left the bar for a minute and we poured ourselves the drink. We knew from that moment on we had experienced something that no one else could come close to."

"That's right, buddy!" Aarik points to Brohn. He then cringes in pain. "Aaaaaaah! It hurts again!"

"Ok, I don't care anymore, I'm doing this," Elliot says.

"NONONONONO!" Aarik shrieks.

"Aarik! I'm not gonna let you die because of some damn whiskey!" Sycilia shouts.

"You don't get it!" Aarik howls. "The flavor profile takes you for a journey. Aaah, the pain! It starts soft on the tongue and you can taste vanilla, and smell tobaccooooooo. Frick frick frick frick friiiiiick... Then it strengthens and you get hit with citrus and leather, and then on the back of the mouth the sweetness crescendos into an absolutely beautiful SHIT! Sorry, a beautiful SHIT!! Damnit, it's a beautiful damn carmel nutty flavor!"

"I taste licorice," Brohn says. "But it's really different for everyone. That's what everyone in the KCW club says."

"You guys joined a club?" Ella asks.

"Can you just get a different spirit please," Aarik begs, "As the guy with the parasite in his leg... oh wait, no... the torso, I would really prefer that."

Elliot looks at Sycilia and Moses, they both shrug, then Elliot turns in absolute astonishment. Moses hits Aarik with a blast of radiant energy again, "That's the last of my pool," He says.

"I guess, get me something else, Hadvar." Elliot says putting the bottle of King's Casket Whiskey on the bar. Hadvar hands him something else. Elliot holds it up: Ragamuffin Mead.

"This good with everyone?"

"That shits strong," Brohn says. "It's almost pure alcohol, so yeah, that's a good choice."

"Are you in a club for that one too?" Ella asks.

"No, I just hang out in a tavern for work. I drink a lot."

"We need to do this now!" Moses says as Aarik begins to scream and writhe again. Elliot runs over, opening the bottle and immediately pouring it on the penetration wound. Hadvar begins to put the Kings Casket back below, but Ella puts her hand out.

"What?" Hadvar asks.

"It's just..." Ella begins, but Gwen takes over.

"After the way they talked about it," Gwen says, "I kinda super wanna taste."

"Yeah, me too," Ella confirms.

"You guys have no idea, it's so good," Brohn says.

"YYYYYEEEEAAAAAH!" Aarik shouts, "It'sss amazing!! Pour me oooooonnnne!"

"How about you focus on keeping that moore worm out of your heart!" Elliot says.

"Hey, for real though, if you're pouring glasses, save one for me," Sycilia says, holding Aariks legs down.

"Seriously?" Elliot looks up at her. She grimaces from the disappointment coming from Elliot's eyes.

"I mean, they made it sound so good," she says.

"Yeah, one for me too," Moses says, holding Aarik's shoulders. Moses looks at Elliot knowing what look to expect. "I'm a paladin, I'm not dead."

Elliot looks between them then pulls out a dagger and slices Aarik's side. "Pour the liquor, if you can keep from drinking for two seconds," he says as he casts several spells around his hands.

"Wow, so judgy," Sycilia says. "Sounds like he needs a drink, too."

Moses pours the spirits over the bleeding wound. "Cover the hole, Sycilia. Cloth or something."

She holds a towel against her brother's torso with one hand and lays her body over his legs.

Elliot begins moving his hands, closes his eyes, and looks as though he's rummaging through something. Aarik screams.

"Sorry bud," Elliot says. "This is just gonna take..." He turns his head, then shifts it again. "There it is." He comes down with his hands and Aarik screams. A deathly and evil moaning comes out of him. "Booze!" Moses pours the mead over the cloth, and the clear, sweet smelling liquor mixes with the blood.

"And... here... we... go!" Elliot says as he yanks his hands back. Aarik jerks and howls. A sudden lump inside Aarik's body shoots out into the towel.

"Wrap it!" Elliot shouts.

Sycilia grabs the creature and wraps it in the wet towel.

"More booze!"

Moses pours alcohol on the creature. It shrieks in agony and squirms in Sycilia's hands. Then it dies.

Elliot pushes Moses' hand toward Aarik's wound. The liquor falls on the hole and Elliot turns. The whole guild is watching him.

"Get me something to drink," Elliot says, defeated.

"One for me, too!" Aarik slurs in his groggy state.

The Penny Lich:

It's a busy time for the Lich. Gwen moves through the open space between tables and candles lit to light the faces of patrons. She swings back and forth with easy grace, as her open coat flaps behind her, and her feet touch softly on the hardwood floors.

"Never say I don't do anything nice for you, boss." She says as she lowers a drink next to Elliot. He smiles and takes a drink, watching her move on. She winks at a customer, and lowers a plate onto the next table for a gentleman. A man belts a singsong tune as he leans on the warm hearth, smoke tickling his lungs from the pipe tobacco.

"What is it that you're asking?" Elliot asks as he sips his drink. The man across the table from him wears a simple shirt, working pants and boots, and a cape wrapped around his shoulders. He pulls out his book and opens it to a map.

"I'm saying, Brother Elliot, that if we can get inside this tomb, then we can learn so much more about Yonder Valley. And we want your guild to be the ones to help us."

Elliot eyes the book. His fingers touch the pages, grasping at the parchment. His skin quivers at the thought of reading the secrets of the tome. The man closes the book and demands Elliot's attention.

"But at the moment," The man continues, "The

Mission of Knowledge is a bit light on coin, and we would be asking to pay you when we find something of value."

"If... I think you mean if something is found," Sycilia says. Elliot breaks his trance and remembers the woman sitting next to him. "You're asking us to work for free. In hopes of getting paid."

"I'm asking you to trust that we are good at our jobs," the man says, his prim hair and clean hands proving that he had not done a hard day's work in some time. He looks through bright brown eyes and taps his hands on the book.

"You're not considering this, are you, Elliot?" Sycilia asks.

"It's a good opportunity to learn more about the valley below," Elliot says, turning to the woman. "There is so much history down there that we still don't know."

"But we need money," Sycilia says. "We can't take free work, especially if it takes us away for weeks at a time."

"Her, I get," the man says. "But you, Elliot of Denier? You're a cleric. You're divinely chosen to do this work. To protect and serve."

"Hey, what do you mean 'her I get'? Man, I'll throat punch you if you say stupid shit like that again."

"She's right," Elliot says, looking at the book. "I appreciate your offer, and if I didn't have my own people to consider, I would go with you in a heartbeat. But I quit the magecore, and I have to figure out my own place in the world now, Brother."

"Brother?" The man stands up. "You're no brother of the church. You're just a mercenary now. A heartless thug with no respect for true knowledge and understanding." He shoves his way out of the busy tavern.

"Yeah, well, you're just a" Elliot stumbles in thought, "-You're a stupid...guy." He looks over at Sycilia, then shouts, "And you're just..."

"Enough, sweety," she says, putting her hand on his arm. "He's gone."

"Yeah, but he's a...a bag of..." Elliot thinks, then stands and shouts, "a bag of beholder dung!" He lowers into his seat, "That's what I should have said."

"You done?"

"Yeah. I think I got him pretty good with that beholder thing."

"Yeah, I'm not sure about that."

Moses, bronze armor clad, and silver glowing eyes approaches the table, letter in hand.

"Have you been contacted by the magecore?" Moses asks, more serious than normal.

"Not really. What's that? A new job?" Elliot looks at the envelope, "Ever since we left," he turns to Sycilia, "the Mistress can't get enough of us."

"Elliot," Moses interjects.

"I mean, I spoke to her maybe once when I worked in the Candle Crypts."

"Elliot, look man..."

"What's a Candle Crypt?" Sycilia asks quickly.

"It's where they keep us scribes. Most clerics are out in the world being heroes, but guys like me get shut up in the ruins just below the temples."

"Sounds awful," Sycilia says.

"Elliot, please," Moses continues to plead.

"It wasn't so bad, hanging out in long dead locations is kinda my thing. it's where Ella and I got married."

"Don't remind me!" Ella says from another table.

"The Mistress didn't even show up- of course- it was illegal and a secret wedding, so I'm kinda glad she wasn't there, but the point is she never cared about me before. But now she cares. Now she wants us to do a new job for her every month or so..."

"They are firing us!" Moses blurts out.

"That was unexpected. But they can't fire us, we don't work for them," Elliot says.

"It's the magecore, all magic users work for them. They're requiring proof of divinity, or the church is releasing our positions," Moses replies.

"That sounds bad," Sycilia says."What's proof of divinity?"

"It's proof that we're doing the work required for us to still be considered Clerics and Paladins."

"You have to like, re-up every few years or something?"

"No," Moses says opening the letter. "The Mistress put a lien out against our titles. Says here that we failed to uphold the church's duties to the magecore, and the church won't back us up and take responsibility for our actions."

"So the church is throwing us under a carriage and the Mistress is driving it. Why would she do this?" Elliot ponders.

"I don't know," Moses says.

"I mean, you guys helped her with that onering smuggling, and I did her stupid festival run. We've only been more helpful as a third party."

"I agree," Moses says. "If you're actually interested in finding out, our hearing is soon. We should probably head over."

"Agreed," Elliot says. He shouts for Gwen, and she gracefully moves toward the owner of the Penny Lich, ready to take his order. "Moses and I are heading out, can you take care of Potsticker? He seems to like you."

"You mean, he likes living in my oven and eating scraps?" she says with a chuckle. "Sure, I can do that."

"Should Aarik and I come with you? Character witness or something?" Sycillia offers.

"No," Elliot says. "Last time you and the Mistress spoke it didn't go well. And Aarik is still recovering from the parasite on our Moonlite contract."

"Oh," Gwen says. "Well, maybe he just needs a good massage. I could, you know, rub him down. If you think, if you, you know, think that would help him. I'm more than happy to do that, for him. And his, toned muscles and soft skin," She fades off in thought. Sycilia snaps her fingers and brings Gwen back.

"You good?" Sycilia asks.

"Yeah. I'll just be going then." Gwen ducks her head low and scampers off. Sycilia turns to the other two and gives them a mildly entertained but confused look.

"You ready to go?" Elliot asks.

"I dunno, I kinda wanna go watch this massage," Moses says, cracking a smile for the first time.

The magecore tribunal office:

The smell of paper and ink fills the air, the sound of several gavels hitting tabletops clamoring. The tribunal office is never as exciting as Moses thinks it should be. He looks around at the hard wood floor and a painting of the first magecore tribunal.

"We lost this," Moses says as Elliot walks up.

"What?" Elliot asks.

"The good old days. When the tribunal was an

example of magecore justice. They used to be a beacon of hope for us who wanted to do things the right way."

"Moses, look at those people in that painting," Elliot says. "They are scorned and jaded by magic." Elliot points to a grim and degenerated man in the painting. His scowl is exacerbated by the scars and battle worn armor. "You want to be that?"

Moses leans in. "Yeesh. Maybe not that guy."

"This is what vengeance looks like."

"Nah, that's what vengeance looks like," Moses says as he points to a regal looking woman. Her upright chin forces her to look down her nose on the audience, and a halo like light shines from behind her. "Look at that form, that posture, that power."

"That's elitism, not vengeance, bro."

"You're so cynical, Elliot. This is the grandmother of the Mistress, she is the matriarch for the entire magecore. She single handedly..."

"Committed genocide," Elliot slips in.

"Helped take back Valeward. She reigned in the chaos."

"By creating antimagic propaganda that led to the death of thousands of glitterbloods."

"You're in a mood," Moses says chuckling. "I get it, you've always been smarter than most, and you see the picture differently than me because of your studies, and whatever Ella did to you. But I think we can both agree that this," he points to the painting, he then finishes by waving his hand to the lobby of the tribunal office, "is better than whatever this has become." The small cubicles with gavels slamming, papers spread out with sins of the defendants on them. Stamps belching out ink and forever condemning men and women to life as a glitterblood offender.

"The world has certainly become heartless," Elliot

says, pushing his glasses up on his nose.

"Are you two ready for your hearing?" a woman says from behind them. They yell in surprise, and turn.

"Where did you come from, woman?" Moses says as he holds his sword slightly out of its scabbard. She looks down at the blade, smiles, and looks back up.

"From behind the painting." She pushes the wall behind the painting and it flops open as a door. "Follow me, they are waiting for you." she disappears behind the door, leaving the two men in awe.

"I mean..." Elliot starts.

"You're gonna have one of these installed at the Penny Lich, aren't you?"

"Hells yes I am."

The Tribunal courtroom:

"Is that Lobstra?" Elliot whispers to Moses. "On the right over there."

"Heh, yeah. I think it is," Moses says. He waves his hand and yells out, "Lobstra! Hey Lobby! It's us, Moses and Elliot, from magecore academy, remember?"

"Silence!" Lico shouts. From the left. Kalevenin the middle slams his gavel down, then looks at the other two for approval.

"Yeesh." Moses whispers, "what is this?"

"The new tribunal council, if I'm not mistaken," Elliot says.

"You stand on trial today," Kaleven begins, "for the right to continue in divine magic properties."

"From the evidence given here, it would seem that you have terminated your connection to the church and its divine right to wield magic." Lobstra continues, "An injunction has been filed against the two of you. What say you to the accusations?"

"You haven't really brought the accusations against us yet," Elliot says.

"Silence!" Lico shouts again.

"No, he's right," Kaleven whispers.

"Also, who is the one that filed our injunction?" Elliot continues. "We have a right to know."

"You have the right to SILENCE!" Lico responds.

"The questions still stand," Moses follows up.

"You have been accused of forfeiting your rank within the magecore to pursue selfish ambitions. As well, one of your new employees is a known magic user who has abused the power of the magecore. Her name is..." Kaleven looks at the paperwork, but Lobstra speaks up without breaking eye contact.

"Elderberry Monroe," she says. "But she is her own issue. You are being brought before the council today due to the nature of your departure. A paladin leaving the magecore to pursue justice is not unheard of, but to set up a guild, for his personal gain, it calls into question his connection to divinity. Even more so, A cleric leaving the church and magecore to run a tavern, a place of ill repute and degradation."

"Who has filed this claim?" Moses asks. "We have a right..."

"I did." A voice calmly says from the side of the room. All eyes turn to see the Mistress standing with her chin held high and her eyes looking down.

"Well, that explains why we got the big room," Elliot says as he watches the Mistress, his old boss, walk to the judge's podium. Lico, Kaleven, and Lobstra look down on the proper woman in the officer's garb.

"Does she wear anything else?" Moses whispers.

"I bet she has officer uniform PJs," Elliot whispers

back. The two chuckle.

"I come before the tribunal judges," the Mistress begins, but never takes her eyes off Elliot and Moses, "to clear up the injunction. There has been a clerical error in this whole case."

"Thank the Divine," Elliot says.

"I never meant for both these men to be brought before you. It was a mistake from the beginning to include them both in this."

"Awesome, she is actually sticking up for us," Elliot says. "I knew we could depend on her doing the right thing. I mean, she always did seem to like us better than the rest of her employees. Right, Moses."

"Aaaaah, I don't know," Moses says, "I have a bad feeling about this."

"What? No," Elliot says. "She's here to clear things up, and we'll be fine. You're so cynical, dude."

"My graces, if you would please be willing to look closer at the injunction," the Mistress continues, "You'll see that the claim is not with Elliot and Moses. but with Elliot of Denier alone. He alone should be stripped of his divine permissions and charged with misuse of a church title."

"What the hells!?" Elliot shouts.

"Oh," Moses says, "I guess you're right, Elliot, everything is gonna be fine."

The Penny Lich:

Sycilia sits alone at her table, near the fire, a glass of ale next to her and papers strewn about. She looks over maps, letters, diagrams and scrolls. Sitting on one of the Penny Lich coasters next to her drink is a wooden ring with small inscriptions etched into it.

She pours over the writing on a letter, not seeing the hand that comes up from under the table. The hand slowly gets closer to fingering the ring. Silently it snakes its way to the jewelry, closer and closer still, shaking in anticipation.

Suddenly Sycilia lets go of her parchment and in a flash brings a dagger down into the hand, pinning it into the wood.

"Good divine! Hollowed Conclave, what the hells!?" a voice comes from under the table. Aarik comes up and looks at his hand in terror. "What have you done!?"

"That's what you get for trying to steal from me."

"You stabbed me!" He points to the blade. "In the hand!"

"Just be happy I didn't cut it off."

"Bro!" Brohn shouts as he comes up from below the table.

"Look what she did," Aarik screams.

"How many of you are under there?" Sycilia asks.

"Wait, she actually stabbed you?! Why?"

"He was stealing from me. No one steals from me," Sycilia says as she pulls the dagger out of his hand. Aarik yelps as the metal unsheathes itself from his flesh.

"I'm your brother," Aarik says.

"So?" she replies.

"I'm your twin. You should have felt that."

"What makes you think I didn't."

"Wait," Brohn pauses, "can you guys actually do that?" They both look at him for a moment.

"Why did you stab your brother, Sycilia?" Hadvar says walking over.

"He was trying to take my evidence?"

"I wasn't!" Aarik says. "I mean, yeah I was trying to stealthily retrieve it for my own uses."

"That's stealing," Sycilia says.

"No, it's not."

"No, it's one hundred percent stealing," Hadvar adds.

"Ok, fine I was trying to steal it." Aarik gives in. "But not 'cause I'm like, trying to be a thief. I just wanted to study it."

"Why would you want to study it," Hadvar begins. "Don't you understand how dangerous this stuff is? Magic isn't something you should be playing with."

"Trust me, Hadvar," Aarik says, "I know how dangerous magic is. I've been studying it since the academy, and I've seen what it's capable of."

"So have I, son," Hadvar says, pointing to the ring. "I saw what those things can do, and before that I saw magic up close and personal in the revolution. My friends laid down their lives, and it was all because of mag-"

SLINK, SLAM! The dagger in Sycilia's hand slices down and stabs Aarik's hand again. His fingers only inches from the wooden ring.

"FLAPJACKIN FLIPFLAP!" Aarik screams, then continues to hiss as his hand writhes in pain.

"Don't try to take my stuff, Aarik," Sycilia says sternly.

"That's both my hands!" Aarik says. "I'm an archer. You've ruined me."

"Serves you right," Hadvar says, "for being tempted by this junk."

"Hush now," Sycilia says. "Gwen's got all her little potions. I'm sure she has something that can help you."

"Her potions aren't for healing," Hadvar says.

"Either way, she'll take care of you until Elliot comes back," Sycilia says.

"Oh, please no," Aarik says, trying to pull the dagger out. "She's crazy. She 'rubbed me down' earlier, and it was like her hands were on fire."

"She'll take good care of you, buddy," Brohn says. "And it seems like your sis won't let this go, so I'm gonna bounce."

"What?" Aarik pleads, "You're just gonna leave me here like this. I thought we were friends, Brohn."

"Yeah. sure. But also, I don't want to get stabbed by your sister."

"FINE RUN!" Aarik shouts as Brohn leaves. "You and I are finished, you hear me! No more late night ice cream conversations, or camp out cuddles. No more thumb wrestling tournaments and you can forget about me rubbing your body down with lotion at the beach!"

"Wow, you guys did all that?" Sycilia asks. "didn't you guys just become friends, like, two days ago?"

"A guy can dream, sis. Please pull this dagger out," Aarik says. Sycilia, never taking her eyes off him, again, pulls the dagger out of his hand. Aarik looks at his bleeding wounds, whimpers, and looks back at Sycilia. She rolls her eyes and stands up.

"Let's get you bandaged up, and Gwen can make you some food. How does that sound? Hadvar, would you mind packing this stuff up so it's safe?"

"ME?!" the bartender reacts. "Why me?"

"'Cause you hate magic, you're the least likely to do anything with it. 'Cause right now, Hadvar, you're the only one I can trust," Sycilia says as she walks Aarik into the back. Hadvar looks at the magic onering on the parchment. Something stirs inside him.

The tribunal court room:

"How have I misused the divine permissions?!" Elliot demands, walking toward the Mistress. A guard puts his hand on Elliot's shoulder, and the cleric rethinks his approach. But speaks past the man, "Name one time I misused the church's power!"

"Since you were in the magecore academy, and even in the temple school, you have been an associate of Elderberry Monroe, have you not?" the Mistress asks knowingly. "And I believe there was an incident some years ago with Miss Monroe and a demon?"

"Ok, name one other time," Elliot gives in.

"Elliot was tricked by Ella," Moses speaks up. "You only know about the incident because he ratted himself out. He filled out his own citation."

"Only at your request, isn't that so, Mr. Summerhill?" The Mistress redirects her attention. "It seems that a cleric should be of greater moral fiber than to be tricked into breaking the law, and then persuaded to do the right thing afterward."

"Hey, I have fiber morals!" Elliot snaps.

"That's not what happened and you know it. Why are you doing this, Ma'am?" Moses begins approaching, the same guard puts his hand on Moses' shoulder. Moses pushes it off and continues. "Elliot and I worked for you for years. I wouldn't be half the paladin I am without his guidance and knowledge."

"My reasons don't matter. What matters now is when the judges declare him unfit for divine permission, Elliot will no longer be a Cleric of Diener."

"Good thing it's up to them and not you," Elliot says. "They know the laws, and they are sworn to upho-"

"GUILTY!" Lico shouts.

"Come on!" Elliot says.

"Hey!" Moses says to Lobstra, "Look, I know you're new and you need to prove yourself as the tribunal of the magecore, but if you cast your verdict now, you are breaking the law. Lobstra, we know you, and we're not looking for special treatment. We know that you were one of the best students of the law—of justice. I looked up to you. You're all here for a reason. You have been called to be the law.

"Elliot has been informed of the litigation against him, but according to the law, he has one week to prove his case for divine permission. If you cast your vote before those eight days are up, then you will begin your careers as unjust figure heads being used by women like her." He points to the Mistress.

Lobster and Kaleven look at each other, then at Lico. "Can I take my vote back, I don't want to be a corrupt lacky." Lico says.

"Elliot of Denier has one week to bring his case to us. If by the eighth day he has yet to prove his continued work for his denomination, then he will be excused from the clergy," Kaleven says. "Go, and prepare yourself for our judgment." He bangs his gavel. Guards lead Elliot and Moses out of the tribunal courtroom, and they can hear as they leave, "Kaleven, that was impressive." Lico says.

"I know, right? Gave me goosebumps."

The Penny Lich:
Sycilia and Gwen sit at the bar with a drink, while Aarik sleeps in a robe on a comfy chair next to the fire. Several other patrons sit and conversate as the day begins to sink into drinking hours. The scent of stew fills the air as dinner begins. Brohn cleans glasses, listening to the conversations.

"Well, I appreciate you buying me some time. I'll start packing tonight and head out in the morning," Elliot says as he sits at a table.

"What? Where are you going?" Sycilia asks.

"The Mistress, or should I say the MistrASS - hehe- is getting me fired."

"Mistrass?" Gwen chuckles, not laughing with him.

"He's been thinking of that the whole way home." Moses says.

"How is she getting you fired?" Sycilia asks. "You don't work for her."

"That's what I said! What are those? Shooting wine?" He leans over and takes both the ladies' wine glasses. He proceeds to gulp them down as Gwen responds.

"No, they're just regular glasses of wine."

Elliot puts both glasses on the bar, a red mustache around his lips. He hisses, "Shooting wine. For the girl on the go."

"Elliot, where are you going?"

"I don't know, and neither can you. That's the whole point, cause in eight days," he turns to Brohn, who refills the glasses and slides them far from Elliot. "That's one whole week there Brohnasourus rex, two shots of your finest! Then, I will be recalled to Lobster's court, and she'll have Kale and Licorice judge me as unsuitable for clerical work. Then the magecore will lock me up for misuse of divine power."

"They can't do that."

"They can and they will. This is what happens when you just quit your job and start running a bar. But you know what else happens?"

"What?" Gwen says.

"You get the chance..." He leans in close to Sycilia, his breath quivering, her eyes watching his, he stum-

bles a bit, "To try shooting wine!" He quickly grabs
Sycilia's glass and throws it back.

"Elliot, that's what I've been trying to tell you,"
Moses says, putting Elliot in a seat. "You don't have to
run. We can figure this out."

"What can we figure out, Moses?"

"You are a cleric. If we can prove that you are still
doing your duty to Valeward, then we can show you
have the need to use your divine permission."

"I'm a cleric of knowledge, Moses. I'm a scribe. I go
through books and write things. I'm the most useless
form of a cleric."

"You're not useless," Sycilia says.

Elliot looks at her and flamboyantly moves his
hand. "Sycilia, honey, trust me, ok? If it doesn't have
to do with books and ledgers, I'm useless. I like numbers, always have. My denomination of divine right
is helping keep order for the government, magecore,
guilds, and such. We aren't the warriors of the other
denominations."

"The denomination that Elliot belongs to is specifically created for people who use their minds more
than their muscles," Moses says. He turns to Elliot,
"But that doesn't matter, at least right now it doesn't,
we can find something that will help you prove your
worth."

"He just needs to perform the tasks of a cleric."
Ella says coming around the group to the bar. Moses
reacts to her sudden appearance, flinching.

"Like what?" Sycilia asks.

"Clerics perform rituals for cleansing, coming of
age, healing, weddings." Ella says. " And depending
on their denomination they can be more specific, the
death clerics of the Sanguine Valley actually do hu-
man sacrifice to the go-"

"Wait, you can perform weddings?" Gwen asks.

"Oh, yeah, no I was done talking." Ella says.

"Have you ever done a wedding?" Gwen pushes Elliot.

"When the mood strikes me," Elliot says through a squished cheek.

"Well, it just so happens that I have a friend who needs an officiant to get married."

"A wedding!" Sycilia says. "Yes!"

"I dunno guys, remember when I said I had done a wedding before, yeah I lied," Elliot says unmoved. "When I took the wedding ceremony class, I puked everywhere. Also, love is stupid."

"Love is not stupid, Elliot," Sycilia says. "And I'm sure you'll do fine. You've done so many cool things since you were in the academy. I believe in you."

"I really don't know." Moses says. "He's really bad on stage. Elliot really hasn't done much in the way of clerical duties. The one time they let him out of the Candle Crypts, he kinda quit and won a tavern in a duel. I was gonna go find a farm that's being attacked by goblins or something, if he can prove he's protecting people, then everything will work just fine."

"You hear that?" Sycilia says. She puts her hand on Elliot's back and talks to him like a child, "You can either officiate a wedding or fight some goblins. What do you wanna do sweetie?"

Elliot moans from the bar top. "I don't wanna do either."

"Oh, come on," Sycilia says. "For me?"

"Fine." Elliot noncommittally throws his pointer finger toward Sycilia. "I'll do the stupid wedding."

"Great!" Gwen says. "I'll go let the couple know." She turns to grab her glass of wine, but sees Aarik finishing it, "Aarik!"

Aarik pulls the glass away and reveals a red stain on his lip, "What? Elliot made shooting wine sound good!"

The Wedding of Hektor and Luciell Winerose:
The temple where the happy couple intends to be wed is nestled in a lovely vineyard on the southwestern border of Valward. The hilly country provides plenty of privacy for the small vineyards covered in fragrant and dew glistening grapes. Columns of white surround a large raised platform made of marble. The platform acts as the foundation to a small pavilion that looks over a deep ravine and creek.

The smell of berries and alcohol wafts in the air, as sunshine breaks through light clouds. Flags of 'Temple Vineyard' whip softly in the breeze, and people find their way to their seats as music plays.

"We are gathered here today to celebrate the union of these two lovers."

"Don't say lovers," Sycilia says. Elliot looks up from his parchment.

"That's one of the lines it comes with," Elliot says. Sycilia sits on a couch with Ella and Aarik. Gwen works on Elliot's tie.

"What do you mean, it comes with?" Sycilia asks.

"It's a fill-in-the-blank speech. I got it out of my class work books," he replies.

"You're using old homework to prep your speech?" Aarik asks.

"Knowing Elliot, it's probably better than what most cleric come up with nowadays," Ella says. Sycilia stands up and looks over the paper.

"We praise the gods for the day they gave us, 'Gwen's friend'? And when he met, 'Gwen's lady friend'? What is this?"

"I don't know their names. It was a filler until I figured out their names."

"You're going to unite them in matrimony in 10 minutes, and you still don't know their names?" Sycilia asks.

"Hektor and Luciell," Gwen responds getting his tie perfect.

"See? Now I know their names." He looks from Sycilia to Gwen. "Uh, which one is the lady friend."

"Your answers are insane, Elliot," Sycilia continues. "'The Divine gave us marriage as a way to both blank and blank us.' You should have obviously put humble and strengthen. Instead you put humiliate and strain."

"Is that what I put?" Elliot says, looking suspicious. "How did you know it was supposed to be humble and strengthen?"

"Uh," she looks slightly suspicious, "I am a girl. It's what we do. Right ladies?"

Ella nonchalantly replies, "Nope. Not important. Now, if you want to know how to humble an ogre, I can help you out with that. But no, not wedding stuff. Unless, the wedding is a trap for a living strigoi. Those dudes love a good wedding. And if you're looking for a..."

"What about you, Gwen?"

"Oh, sorry no. Didn't fit with li'l Gwen's lifestyle. I don't think people would say I grew up as a normal girl though. So, you know, I'm the weird one."

"It doesn't matter, why I know it, I just know it, and you should too. Why are you acting like this?" Sycilia asks.

"Cause I don't want to do it. I feel like I've been

very clear about this."

"It's true," Aarik agrees with Elliot. "He's been very clear about it."

Moses walks up to the group. "The bride is ready. The groom is waiting. Let's do this."

"Oh, you know what? I think-" Elliot puts his finger to his lips, "I think, I'm not gonna do it."

"You have to," Gwen says.

"They're all waiting on you," Sycilia adds.

"Yeah, except, oh I have to use the bathroom." Elliot feigns.

"Procrastination poop!" Ella says, "He did the same thing at our wedding!"

"That's because I was about to commit a felony!" Elliot says.

"No pooping till after your speech." Sycilia says.

"Ok but,"

"No buts," her finger in his face. She begins moving in toward the podium, "Do your job."

Elliot reluctantly moves into place next to the groom. Hektor stands in his traditional wedding cloak, the headband of matrimony around his head. He smiles at Elliot, and Elliot weakly smiles back.

He then leans in to whisper to Hektor, "Pss," he hisses, "Pssssss."

Hektor looks at him with uncertainty.

"Look man, are you sure you want to do this?" Elliot whispers.

"What?" Hektor asks.

"I mean, like, do you even know this chick? You could be tying yourself down to a lunatic."

"What's wrong with you? Aren't you supposed to be a cleric?"

"I am, I am, but like, not the kind that gives speeches and stuff, so if you wanna just say the wedding... eulogy... thing, that would be great."

"You want me to marry myself and my bride? What kinda cleric are you?"

"I'm just a–" Elliot is interrupted by music. The band plays the traditional wedding waltz that leads the woman down the aisle. Hektor's eyes tear up as he sees his bride walking toward him. Several birds fly overhead and flowers grow before her every step.

"I just think it would be better if you spoke from the heart, you know?" Elliot continues to pester Hektor.

"Can I just enjoy this moment please?"

"Yeah, yeah. Sure." Elliot leans back. Then whispers in his ear, "But where did we land on the whole you doing the speech thing?"

"She's just so beautiful."

"Oh. Ok, so you're just gonna ignore me and pay attention to your bride? Got it."

Luciell makes her way to the podium and takes her groom's hands. They stare at each other for a moment, as the procession quiets down. A moment passes and they turn to see Elliot watching them.

"Right, of course," he says, opening his book. "We are gathered... Huuulg." He holds back the vomit. The crowd watches him, and he can feel sweat pouring out. His stomach lurches in anxiety.

"Sorry," he says waving it off. "We are gathered today to celebrate, Hrrrulg." He turns. The crowd becomes unsettled. Moses runs over to Elliot.

"Bro," Moses says, "You ok?"

"No. I don't do speeches. I hate weddings."

"Come on man. If you want to keep being a cleric, you need to buck up."

Elliot takes a few breaths. "Fine. Let's do this." He turns back to the bride and groom and opens his book again, "Where were we? Ah yes, Celebrate the union of these two...Glaaaaaag!" Vomit erupts from his mouth and splashes onto the witnesses gathered. An arc of green and yellow flows from him.

With dripping goo on his face and his robe covered in vomit, he looks at the two, smiles, and says, "Lovers."

A Road on the outskirts of Valeward:

"So you're still holding on to a lot of trauma from being married to Ella, eh?" Aarik asks as he walks with Elliot.

"What makes you say that?" Elliot pushes his glasses up, and readjusts his backpack.

"The vomit that's still on your neck," Aarik points out.

Elliot quickly wipes his neck, grimaces, and wipes his hand on his cloak. "Yeah, I guess. It's not her, ya know. I almost gave up all my hopes and dreams of being a cleric for her, and she was just using me."

"Do you think she was only really using you? Do you think she has no love for you?"

"I think there's love. I think that's why she is the way she is. Because she loves everyone, and that causes her to be callus toward specific people. She is a hunter, that's what she does, and with the way her brain works, that's all she can focus on. It's not about the room in her heart; it's the room in her head."

"Seems like wise words from a guy that hates love" Sycilia says as she slows down.

"I have to distance myself from it. I don't actually hate love, I just..." He looks at the two of them and sighs. "I guess I'm jealous."

"If you're jealous, then why do you keep fighting to

be a cleric?" Sycilia asks.

"It's who I am. Ever since I was a kid. I mean, I was literally dedicated as a child, left by my mother and father to be this. If I give it up, then it means their sacrifice was for nothing."

"Harsh," Aarik says.

"I know, right?"

"The sun is almost down, We better hurry to the farm. Moses and Ella will be waiting." Sycilia says.

The Farm outside Valeward:

Elliot gets pulled along the road leading to the farm house.

"Come on, Elliot. We need to hurry, Moses is waiting for us, the goblins won't kill themselves." Sycilia says.

"I'll go ahead," Aarik says, his hand outstretched. A puff of black mist shimmers around it. Suddenly a bow takes shape in his fist and he runs.

"What's your deal?" Sycilia says, waiting on Elliot to catch up.

" Well it's dark out, and running at night sounds like a nightmare, also I'm not in very good shape. I mean look at me. You could replace me with a scarecrow, and it'd be as effective."

Sycilia stops and looks at Elliot. "Will you stop doing that?"

"Doing what?" Elliot pulls up and breathes hard.

"Ragging on yourself," she says. "My Divine, you fought a barbarian warlock and won his tavern. You faced a deity, and you're now the father, kind of, to an elemental spirit."

"More like guardian. the father is an actual Elemental Lo–"

"Elliot, you can be whatever you want to be," she continues. "I have seen you do some crazy stuff. And you're running a guild with your best friend. You two are an inspiration. Why do you always doubt yourself?"

"Because it's not me that achieves these things, Sycilia. I don't do anything. I run the finances of the guild and the bar. Moses runs the guild, Hadvar runs the bar. I became Potsticker's guardian because I made a mistake. The Penny Lich is a fluke, and I don't know if I can keep it going. For Divine's sake, you're the reason I even have the Penny Lich. You're the one that actually took on Noodle, not me. Since the moment I met you, I could see greatness in you. You're strong and confident and beautiful." He lets the words settle awkwardly, then picks up, "and I'm reminded that I am a bookworm who was too afraid to do real magic, so I stuck with divine magic."

"What do you mean, real magic?" she asks.

"The wizards of Valeward were some of the greatest minds in the kingdom. Growing up, I always idolized them. Freda Talimoni, Scrivner the Scaly Scribe, Garnision the Great. I wanted to do magic like them. But I lived at the temple. I was dedicated to the Divine. Rather than become a mighty warrior and defender of my Denomination, I focused on books, and stories, and lore."

"No wonder Ella liked you."

"Yeah. I don't know if she actually liked me, or liked the idea of learning more about long dead dragon kings and werewolves. But even then, as soon as the church saw my love of books, they put me in that damn magecore basement and I was stuck. The only adventure I got was from reading about the Sentry Valley, or hearing Moses' stories. I was thrown away,

Sycilia. I wasn't brave enough to choose what I wanted, and I wasted my life on the shit I couldn't live up to."

"Hey," Scycilia says as she puts her hand on his shoulder. "You're not in the Candle Crypts anymore. You may not have put the sword to Noodles throat, or purposely called forth the avatar of a fire plane deity. Yeah, you have a hard time with fear, and giving speeches, and confrontation in general."

"And seaweed."

"You're scared of seaweed?"

"Is it a plant? We don't know! It could be alive when it's in the water, and then just die on land!"

"That's not the point, Elliot," She continues. "The point is, you did do something. You quit your job because you knew that you could do more by going out into the world. You chose that. I will never forget you choosing Aarik and I over the magecore. If you want to continue to be a cleric, then you need to buck up and get to the fight."

Elliot looks at her for a moment, then at the road. "No, I left the Candle Crypts to be a better man. And giving up on being a cleric because it's too hard is not the man I want to be." Elliot limps forward majestically, pumping his good leg forward and using his bad one to stabilize himself as he pushes his staff into the ground. Heroically, he moves toward the fight with the goblins. The sweat and tears meld together into a physical manifestation of his great effort.

"Elliot, why are you limping?" Sycilia asks, watching him from behind.

"Cause it looks more epic." The music swells in Elliot's head.

"Stop. You look moronic," She pushes him into run.

They come around the bend to the farmstead, the field of corn to one side, as a large barn breaks out of the vegetation. A tall house stands in the fresh moonlight, overlooking a field of grass and hay bales.

And in front of the barn, Moses stands before a pile of dead goblin bodies. Aarik puts an arrow into one of the goblin's heads. Ella jumps down from a tree. She is covered in blood and readies a bolt in her crossbow. She turns to see Elliot and Sycilia, points her crossbow at them and pulls the trigger.

They hold their breath as the bolt flies between them and lands in the head of a goblin in a tree behind them. He falls as a croak of failure leaves his body and he dies.

"You guys are late," Ella says.

"Apparently," Sycilia says.

"We couldn't wait," Ella continues, "Moses said we had to defend them even if you weren't here."

"Elliot, man," Moses says, cleaning his sword and sheathing it. "Where have you been? You mis–"

"Missed it, I know," Elliot says. "And now I can't prove that I'm worthy of my magic. Damn it. This is why I don't get my hopes up."

"Well, we can just say you did it," Aarik says, as he walks up. "No big deal."

"Moses won't lie for me. And I wouldn't ask him to," Elliot responds, as he looks over the dead bodies.

"Nah, I can do it." Moses says. "I want to help you, Elliot."

"Really?" Elliot says, astonished. "You would do that for me?"

"Absolutely." Moses says.

"Oh, Paladin Moses! Our Hero!" A woman's voice shouts from the house. "We saw the whole thing from up in our bedroom. Ya're The Divine's own warrior you are." The whole family comes running up to shake his hand and pat him on the back.

"The way you and your two friends here took on all those goblins, truly heroic work, I'd say."

"You always have a seat at our table, Paladin Moses. Thank you for your work tonight."

"Oh, look, a cleric of the church is here, he must have been hiding in the bushes, waiting for Moses to finish his work."

"Here to send these goblins' bodies back to where they belong, eh Cleric?"

"Now that your Paladin has done all the work, you can get started on yours, eh? Don't worry, we'll let the church know you both did your parts. Paladin Moses fought the monster off, and his cleric...assistant, cleaned up the bodies."

"Thanks." Elliot says, defeated, and emotionless. The family leads Moses into the house where the smell of cooked meats and baked breads roll out into the night air. Elliot's face doesn't change as the world around him strips away and he finds himself at the Penny Lich once again. Several glasses of wine in front of him.

Several days later:
"I'm a little concerned about him. He's been shut in his office for several days," Gwen says as Moses sits at the bar.

"I've been trying to get him to come out, but he says that he's never coming out, which seems insane. He has to eat and drink."

"Dad's been sliding food in under the door. Says he's not the first crazy owner of the Lich."

"What about a bathroom? Dude needs to move

those bowels at some point."

"Prestidigitation," Ella says sitting at a table with Aarik and Sycilia.

"Gross." Aarik says.

"What?" Moses asks.

"Prestidigitation." Ella says again. "It's a basic spell, most mages use it as a practice spell or to make a quick buck."

"Some," Aarik adds, "will even clean clothes with it. The spell is capable of just kinda, magiking away dirt and grime and stuff."

"So you're saying he's just kinda..." Moses starts to put things together. He moves his hands like a bowel movement, then waves his hand, and makes a disappearing motion. "That?"

"Probably," Ella says.

Moses trudges over to the door. "Hey! Elliot, it's your hearing date! You need to buck up and we need to figure this out!"

No answer.

"Elliot, come on man, you're my best friend. If you can't do it, then I'll help you. That's what we do right? We help each other."

Silence.

"Screw you! I never wanted to help anyway." He moves aways from the door in a huff, then back to it. "I'm sorry about that buddy, I didn't mean that. I'm just so scared, you know, of losing you, of losing what we have."

The guild watches in confusion. "Are they, like... together?" Sycilia asks Ella.

"They are very close," Ella replies.

"Yeah, sis. Guys can be close, it doesn't have to be weird, just cause it doesn't fit your gender normative expectations."

Moses yells at the door again, "If you're going to treat me like this then why don't you just prestidigimon poop into your mouth!" He starts to walk away, but immediately turns back and starts to stroke the wood and talk real close, "I'm sorry, buddy. It's just a stressful day, but I wanna make it all good for you, you know like the day at that carnival?" Moses giggles, "You remember that, do you?" Giggles some more, "Yeah you do, we were so naughty that day, remember?"

The guild continues to watch.

"OK," Aarik says, "That's weird."

Several minutes later Moses comes to the bar and looks at the guild. "I'm going to go to Elliot's trial, whether he wants to go or not. Someone here needs to protect him, and since I'm a paladin, I'll do my job. If he emerges, please let him know where I'll be." And with that Moses walks off.

"I feel kinda bad for them." Aarik says.

"Why?" Ella asks.

"They've been best friends forever, and it was always 'cause they wanted to achieve something. Now It seems like they're gonna break up."

"They won't break up over this," Ella says confidently.

"No?" Aarik questions.

"Nah. After Elliot and I broke up, he and Moses became even closer. They love each other. In some ways I think Elliot loves Moses more than he ever loved me."

"Sure," Aarik says, "but you two broke up specifically because you two wanted different things out of life. I mean, just look at it this way, Elliot broke the law to marry you, that's how much he loved you. Moses and Elliot aren't married, they have no attachment, it will be even easier for him to leave."

Before Ella even realizes what is happening, she's at the door. It's locked, but she pulls out a small strip of paper covered in runes. She wraps it around the door handle and speaks a quick word and hears it unlock.

The room isn't what she expected.

Instead of a room in disrepair, with poop staining the walls, she finds a proper and well kept office.

"What do you want, Ella?" Elliot says without looking up from his book.

"This place is clean, I expected to find everything a mess."

"I've been stress cleaning," Elliot says.

"And stress reading?" Ella asks.

"'The duty of the cleric is to be a representation of the Deities, as they are for the Divine. The servants of the Avatars.'" He looks up at her. "I have read that sentence a hundred times. I can't get past it."

"It's just foundational understanding given to us by the Virgil Empire. I think you can move past it," Ella says. "It's doctrine from an Empire that we kicked out over a century ago."

"That's not the point."

"What is the point?"

"This is what I was born to do. This is who I've always been."

"But it's never really been who you want to be," Ella says matter-of-factly.

"And who do I want to be, Ella? It definitely wasn't a monster hunter, like you. Or a warrior like Moses."

"And It's more than the guy asking for magic leftovers when he should be the one making the rules. Elliot, I know that being Fey Touched means everyone thinks you're half-mad, and unattached. But I see you for who you really are. You're pure of heart, and you're too smart to waste your life not diving weird shit. That's why I always loved you. Because you wanted to know more, and it was always to help the people around you. There was nothing better than diving into the secrets of long dead mages and kings with you, cause you made it fun."

Elliot looks up at her. An idea begins to form in his head, and he smiles as it sets in. "Ella, if I didn't know you better, I would kiss you."

"You'd try."

"I have to go. I just realized something."

"Yeah, I can see that."

"Promise me something."

"What, Elliot?"

"Promise me you won't disappear again," Elliot says as he gathers his books and leaves through the door. "Potsticker! Come with me!"

The Magecore Courtroom:

"And where is the defendant?" Kaleven the Judge asks. Moses steps forward, and speaks.

"Well, my lord, Elliot is actually detained at the moment."

"From his own hearing?" Lico asks indignantly.

"What reason does he have for not being here?" Lobstra asks.

"Well, that's the thing. So, he's not here because, he's actually in the middle of, eh," Moses stalls, trying to think of anything to say, "he had...a bad egg."

"Wha?" Kaleven asks.

"A bad egg," Moses grabs onto the excuse. "A really bad one. Rotten to the core, you know. And now it's just puke, and poop, and snot and the whole works."

"Gross," Kaleven says.

"I doubt that very much," Lobstra says .

"Do you want to take a chance, Lobstra?" Kaleven says, "The man could be here right now getting sick all over the place. No, no indeed."

"It doesn't matter," Lico says. "He isn't here and that means his role as cleric is forfeit, and he will be arrested for misuse of divine power." Lico brings his gavel up.

"Wait!" Elliot's voice calls out from the doors. Lico looks up and rolls his eyes at the new addition. "I have some pertinent information for the council."

"Guards! Seize him!" Kaleven screams. "And if you sense him about to puke, take him outside immediately."

"He's not going to puke, Kaleven," Lobstra says. "You're not going to puke, right?" She turns to Elliot.

He shakes his head at her. "No, I don't plan to."

"Planning and doing are two different things!" Kaleven begins to throw out. "Guards, does he smell like running brown? Is he sanitary?"

"I'm fine," Elliot says as he approaches the podium. "I apologize for my tardiness."

"We're glad you're here to speak for yourself, Elliot," Lobstra says. "But I have to admit, I'm concerned you and Moses here don't take these charges seriously."

"That's not true, Lobst—your Honor," Elliot begins. "I spent this last week trying to figure out what it is I do, and what I want to do. Are they the same thing? Am I capable of doing what I want, or am I stuck doing something that is expected of me? I realized something: life is about the balance of these two things.

"I love what the church does. I love that I'm a part of a community of people that helps others—hat we

---

exist to lift up the world around us. Even in my small way, I can contribute to that. Sure, I can't fight monsters or give speeches. I'm not good at a lot of things. And because of that I was shut away in the Candle Crypts and used by the Mistress to run her books. Record the stories of other clerics who would go out on heroic quests, or paladin's who kept order. I would do numbers and find ways to become more efficient. I would research the past of this city—this kingdom. But in that, I found a longing for something more: magic. Real magic. I learned about its past, its capabilities, and the true nature of it. I hid this part of me away, and I only let it out when I knew I could get away with it. Learning about it, spending years in the libraries and scrolls, I learned as much as I could."

"That's great, Elliot," Kaleven says. "But all you're telling us is that you read some books. What does that have to do with you leaving to become a bar owner."

"Because I finally broke out!" Elliot says. "I finally saw what it was like to be in the world. I was tired of hearing my friend's stories." He looks at Moses. "And I was ready to start living them."

"But what have you done to prove you're a cleric? If you're not in the Candle Crypts, what good are you?" Lico asks.

"First of all, ouch, that hurts, secondly," Elliot begins, then whistles, "This!" At the moment, bounding into the chamber, is a creature made entirely of fire, whose body looks like a flame. His feline face sniffs the air and he looks around. Seeing Elliot, he runs up and starts to rub up on his leg. Elliot picks him up and shows him off. "This is Potsticker."

Lobstra and one of the female guards both let out an awe whimper, but are quick to compose themselves.

"Potsticker is the child of a Fire Elemental lord and the Deity Astra. He represents the chaotic nature of something or other. Honestly, it's been a month or so since I spoke to Astra, and I don't remember. But she chose me to care for and raise her child. It is my duty, appointed by the Hallowed Conclave, to teach this creature how to be a proper avatar. I have been chosen!" Elliot holds Potsicker up, who takes a regal and heroic pose as well.

"So you're willing to abandon everything you've sworn to do and uphold, just so you can galavant around with a pitcher of ale?" Lico asks. "And you justify it by having a fire demon in your possession?

"No. I never said I'd give up on what the church has taught me, or what I find useful for the church. I quit the magecore reclaimers, not my faith in my community." Elliot pulls out several papers from a scroll case, "I made a stop on the way here, and I spoke with The Mission of Knowledge. After looking over their proposal for the excavation of the Southern Valley Temple, I have decided to fully fund the venture through the proceeds of the Penny Lich. And I will be accompanying them on the trip down to supervise the beginning of the expedition. And with any luck, I will find some new information that can be brought back and given to the Church as proof of my divine permission."

"You're going to travel into the frontier of Yonder Valley and explore an ancient temple? With your little fire boy?" Lobstra asks, eyes wide in disbelief.

"Yes, ma'am," Elliot says confidently.

"You're going to take on lethal traps and magiks forgotten about, all so you can justify your place in the church?" Lico asks.

"Y... yes, sir." Elliot says less confidently.

"You're going to travel for months, go into a maze-like underground structure that can collapse at any moment, filled with monsters and molds, and darkness that this world has not yet seen?"

"I mean," Elliot thinks for a second, "yeah, tha'ts the plan."

"You?" Moses says, in as much shock.

"Yes." Elliot says in irritation. He turns back to the tribunal, "I have realized that I can do both. I can continue to uphold the expectations you have for me, while still living the life I want to live. And if you decide to deny me my permissions, then you'll know where to find me." Elliot smiles as he finishes the thought, Postciker on his shoulder. "In the ruins of an ancient dragon king!"

The Magcore graveyard:

A massive arching iron gate stands between the people of Valeward and the wizard's graveyard. Its proximity to the eastern marshes causes an almost unending fog, as darkened and wicked trees grasp at the air. A heavy scent of decay fills the nose.

Hadvar looks at the graves through the bars of the iron fence. The memories of his friends come rushing back at him. The reality of magic, war, and death. His comrades disintegrated as they get hit by beams of energy. Corruption filled their blood and turned them to black goo. His stomach drops as he feels the terror once again.

The gate opens on its own, and Hadvar watches it. Slowly he makes his way to the gate. The long squeal ends and Hadvar passes through. The mist pulls him in, coiling around his body.

He passes gravestone after gravestone as he walks down the old cemetery cobblestone. He pulls the hood over his head and becomes a shadow like the ghosts that haunt him. His silhouette is a floating black spector winding its way down toward the mausoleum in the center.

"Have you any news, Hadvar?" a voice says in the mist.

Hadvar stops and looks up at one of the statues looming out of the gloom. It stands in mage robes, holding a staff of power.

"Or are you simply here to damn these glitterblood spirits."

"Still hiding in the shadows, eh Grimander?" Hadvar asks.

"You might have gotten everyone to believe you're different from the Hadvar I knew back in the day," the voice says, "but we both know that people don't really change, do they?" With that, a figure in a dark cloak appears in front of Hadvar, his tall silhouette obscured by the veil around him.

"She said you had come back. I didn't believe her," Hadvar says.

"You shouldn't. Fact is, I never left."

"Then where have you been? Where did you go after the Fall of Onyx?"

"I had some loose ends to tie up. But we have a bigger problem."

"That's what she was telling me. It can't be true, can it?"

"It is. But what I need from you is information. What has the Penny Lich crew discovered."

"Oh, I see. You're still worried about him, eh? Your precious little trinket maker. Well here." Hadvar flicks the onering that Sycilia gave to him. It spins in the air and the figure catches it with a flick of his wrist. "Waller. It's his work. And the bandit that was buying from him said his name. According to this girl's research."

"So he's in hiding. But he's still making things. That's good for us."

"Good for you maybe," Hadvar says. "I'm not a part of your crew any more. I just needed to see you with my own eyes. I needed to know after all these years, that you were still as selfish as I thought you were back then."

"That's too bad, Hadvar." The figure in the dark says. Suddenly he emerges directly in front of Hadvar. Standing a foot taller than the man, the black cloak covering him completely. He looks down and whispers soft words that float on the misty air. "With what's coming, I figured you might want a way to keep you and your daughter safe. How is she by the way? Has she met her mother yet?"

"I knew this was a bad decision. Goodbye, Grimander." Hadvar turns away, but as he does the figure appears in front of him again.

"Take it, then, as a parting gift. And a thank you for helping us one last time." The figure's gloved hands hold a book inches from Hadvar's body. It is a leather bound book, with a symbol engraved in the hard surface. The symbol is a triangle pointing downward, and three circles inside of it, each inside another one. Hadvar's eyes widen. His hands reach out, but they stop short.

"It's ok, old friend. It is yours, I only held onto it for your protection," Grimander says. Hadvar looks up at the blackness of the figure's featureless face. He chews on his tongue, squints his eyes, and takes the book.

T.W. CLAWSON

THE PENNY LICH

A FANTASY SITCOM

Witcher?

I hardly know her.

The Penny Lich in the evening.

Torches burn throughout the building. Glass lanterns flicker in synchronized patterns. The dancing light falls on the tables and faces of patrons. A happy song makes its way through the Penny Lich on a busy evening. The wooden bar and shelves of alcohol are surrounded by several people eager to give Brohn their money.

Hadvar works diligently on his famous boar ribs, allowing scented smoke to waft throughout the building and into the street, which tempts passers-by to part with their coin. Hadvar whistles a tune in the back, as a bard takes a small stage next to the fireplace and sings her tavern songs. Moses speaks with several patrons about what the Penny Lich Guild offers, giving them each small hardened bits of parchment with magic runes on them.

"No, no, this is magecore sanctioned, I promise you. See here: Moses Summerhill Paladin at law," he says pointing to his name on the stiff bit. "And yes, if you use this calling card, then you can reach out to me in any moment of emergency. Give me your location and a quick description, and me and/or my team will be happy to assist." He pats the man on the shoulder and nods.

A new jaunty melody starts and Moses picks up his mug and cheers with the small group he's with.

Brohn and Ella chat while Brohn makes cocktails
and pours drinks from the bar. Ella draws on a parchment, explaining the structure of a polyamorous werewolf relationship, and the reason why it's important
to know it. At nearby tables, patrons talk in delight
about the sweet smell of pork meat spilling throughout the large gathering place. Salivation and merri-
ment mix into a festive evening at the Penny Lich.

Then Ashley walks in.

Boots made of black leather, moving up the calf and
laced tight up to the thigh. Her pants are tucked in. A
belt of leather wraps around her waist and both legs in
several conflicting orbits. A vest of black leather and
ornate silver stitching is pulled tight by many black
leather buckles. She wears a red blouse, with long
crimson sleeves running over her perfectly toned arms
into silver gauntlets. A dented and petite pauldron
covers her left side, while a crimson and black cape
drapes over her right side.. There's some more leather
wrapped around her neck to hold the cape, and then
probably a little more leather in places no one can
see, and then some leather pouches attached to some
leather rings attached to a leather belt, and finally a
black and red leather hat. She has a common theme.

She pulls the wide brimmed tri-pointed hat off her
short asymmetrical curly hair, and she peers out from
behind rose colored spectacles.

"So you were saying that for any reason at all, I can
use this and call you?" The patron speaking to Moses
says, unaware of the women that entered the tavern.
Moses on the other hand notices her, and immediately
stands. As the man speaks, Moese puts his finger on
the man's lips and shushes him.

"I was just saying to my wife, we could realmshm-
mm."

"Shuuuuuush." Moses puts his whole hand on the man's face, pushing him away. He continues to walk forward, never taking his eyes off the woman. She looks around for a moment, sees him, and nods, eyeing him up and down.

Moses approaches and touches his head band and bows slightly. "Ma'lady." He immediately regrets saying it and stays bowed.

"Hello Paladin Moses," she says. "My name is Ashley Vandorren. I am with the Aberrant Hunters League. We came here looking for you and your business partner. Would you care to buy me a drink and talk business?"

Moses wonders why such a wildly gorgeous woman has come into the world to find him. And also that he's still bowing. It's been too long of a bow. He needs to straighten up and introduce himself. He begins to straighten up, and even begins to introduce himself. But then he realizes, she's already said his name, he doesn't need to introduce himself. He needs to acknowledge her rank and position. So then he decides to say that instead. But she asked him a question, in the order of conversational operations, one should always answer the question then get back to the original point made. So he'll go ahead and answer the question.

Of course all this comes out as he shoots straight up and begins to speak while changing his mind. So Ashley Vandorren watches a Paladin bow to her, then suddenly shoot up at attention, and shout, "Hi'm Moses Sumnice to meet you Ms. Vanorder up a cocktail on me!" This is of course very funny, obviously, so Moses figures he'll break the tension by laughing, but having just spoken a greeting without breathing, he finds himself out of breath and his only laugh is a wheeze and gurgle of the throat.

Ashley watches in mild entertainment as the paladin finishes his gurgling laugh and swallows his spit down. Mose sucks in air and swallows again. Breathing hard for a second, he looks back up at her.

"So that drink?" she asks.

"Yeah, right over here." Moses leads her to the bar. He flashes two fingers to Brohn and quickly gets two shots.

"I was told by the magecore that you and your business partner, Elliot the Cleric, are running a Guild that focuses on the needs of the people. Is that true?"

"Yes," Moses says taking both shots before she can reach for one of them. Moses signals to Brohn again, this time Brohn pours them and places them in front of Ashley.

"I would like to hire you for a job, if you're not busy." Ashley puts her hat on the bar. She turns to see Ella eyeing her.

"Crimson Tribunal," Ella says.

"Blood for blood," Ashely says. Ella nods and Ashley turns back to Moses. "You have a hunter in your employ?"

"We have Ella, yes. She, I guess, eh, she does some stuff every once in a while. We keep her around for the weirdos and freaks, you know. When we need to get our hands dirty, " Moses waffles.

"What's the job?" Ella asks. Brohn comes close and cleans several glasses.

She looks at the three of them, and smirks. "Well, I went to the magecore with an aberrant murder, but because the people found dead were commoners, no one sees a need to investigate."

"Classic magecore mindset," Moses says, "That's exactly why we started the Penny Lich Guild."

"I thought it was the People's Guild," Brohn says.

"Well, I mean it is, technically," Moses says, "But since we formed here, and hang out here, and one of the founding members owns the bar, we have just kinda come to be known as the Penny Lich Guild." Moses looks back to Ashley. "Sorry, we're still figuring things out here, you'll have to excuse a few wavering bits of information as we get our feet under us."

"Sure. anyway, someone mentioned your guild, and so I want to hire you to help investigate the murder, which I believe has been perpetrated by a witch."

Ella's eyes grow wide.

"A witch you say?" Ella gets between Moses and Ashley. "What kind of witch? A hag? A green hag? A hedge witch? A brujeria? Oh, could it be a barovi–"

Moses pushes her out of the way.

"Excuse me. Excuse me!" Moses says fighting for his spot back. Ella slaps Moses, Moses slaps her back, and they trade soft blows for a moment, before Ella backs off.

Moses clears his throat, "So a witch you say?"

"Why wouldn't the magecore be interested in a witch running loose?" Ella asks, staying as close to Moses as she can. "If there's magic running around unchecked, they usually get involved immediately."

"Well, to be honest. They don't think it was magic." Ashley takes a shot. "The scene is gruesome and the magecore investigators have said that it was the attack of a wild beast. They have put the Green Cloaks in charge of the investigation."

"Ok, so they have rangers looking into it. But you think there's more to it," Moses says.

"Exactly. I've spent my life hunting aberrants, sorcerers, witches, and shadow mages. I know what it looks like when they unleash their power." Ashley pulls out a cloth covered in blood. "And if I'm right, then I can't take this thing on alone. Which is why I'm coming to you for help."

The Investigation begins:
The northeast part of Valeward, before the King's Wall and marshes, is an area populated by commoners and beggars. The streets are broken by dirt patches and weeds. Buildings tower and lean in the air, some half collapsed into other buildings. The warmth of fire hides behind closed windows and doors. A thin layer of water lines the gutters, where the wooden buildings give off an odor of rot.

Tents propped on the streets add to the clutter of unwanted litter that has been cast aside. The trash and its people sleep in damp shelters. Some look down on the streets from the rooftops, their shelter being the tarps pulled over chimneys and clothes lines.

"You ok?" Moses asks Brohn as they walk through the moonlit streets.

"Hmm?" Brohn breaks from his thoughts.

"You seem a little distracted. You ok?" Moses repeats.

"Yeah, Just didn't think I'd come back to the Grindstone District anytime soon."

"You're from here?"

"Yeah." Brohn points to a small shack as they pass by. "I lived there." He points to another spot. "And there. This is where most orphans end up. Families here take them in and use them to make extra coin."

"But you found a home eventually, right?"

"Unfortunately."

"You'd rather live here on the streets?"

"I'd rather not be used. And I'd rather children not have to choose between the streets and fighting in illegal fighting rings."

"My divine." Moses stops. "Is that what happened to you?"

Brohn throws on a fake smile and chuckles a little. "It's fine man. I made it out, right? We have a job to do. Let's do it."

"Well, I'm glad I didn't eat before we came here. Would have been a waste of a meal," Ella says as the two men walk into the room. She and Ashley are looking over the crime scene.

"Come on, Ella, have a little sympatheeeeeoooo, my Divine!" Moses' mouth is agape as he steps into a horror scene.

"What fresh hell realm is this!?" Brohn half screams out. He puts his hands out but immediately touches blood on the walls. He turns and slips, catching himself and grabbing an intestine. They both notice that two bodies have been torn apart and spread about the room. And because it's so gross, It's best explained by Ashely.

"The victims were Carl and Cynthia Beats. They're bodies were torn from the inside out. Notice the wound?"

Moses looks at one of the exposed parts of the skull on the woman, "Hard to miss," he grimaces. "Almost like the fissure protruding outward on the skull is pushing outward."

"Like a popcorn kernel," Ella says as Brohn gags.

"Exactly," Ashley continues. "You can see legs and feet stayed intact with the abdomen,"

"Except for the diastasis that begins at the end of this piece here." Moses bends down to look at a part of the body.

"You can see in the bed are severed fingers. Over here is an arm," Ella points out.

"And I believe in this corner is, ah yes, the other arm." Ashley points to an arm right next to Brohn's head. "You'll see that they were both disemboweled, but the odd part again is the wound looks more like a tearing."

"Jagged and pulpy," Moses says as Brohn holds his hands over his mouth. "Something tore into these people."

"Which is why my colleagues believe this to be an animal attack. But again, you'll notice on the remaining intact flesh that the lacerations on both sides have subdermal hematoma."

"Stretching?" Ella asks.

"What are you three saying?" Brohn asks. "And can you all stop acting like this isn't disgusting?"

"This is an investigation, Brohn," Ella says.

"The pattern of breakage," Moses continues, "points again to an internal mass breaking out of their bodies." He looks at a chunk of meat covered in blood.

"And this all points to a witch?" Brohn asks, covering his nose and mouth.

"My theory," Ashley begins, "is that a witch cast a spell on these...these two unlucky souls and caused swelling hemotomic tumors-

"Common, please," Brohn says.

"She caused sacks of blood to grow inside them, and they exploded from the inside out."

"Gross!" Brohn says.

"Amazing!" Ella says.

"Interesting," Moses says.

"So you agree with my theory?" Ashley asks, her eyes almost pleading with Moses.

"Well, the blood splatter agrees with you," Ella says. "Or rather, you agree with it. For two common humans, there is too much blood on the walls, and ground, and ceiling, and bed, and dining table. And Brohn." She points to her face while looking at Brohn, and he begins to wipe himself down.

"The real question is, where do we go from here?" Moses asks.

"That's what I was hoping to get your help with," Ashley responds. "Where would a witch go after this? Any ideas on how to track her?"

"Her tracks would have been cleaned by the water on the streets," Brohn says.

"I can only track someone that I've seen," Moses adds.

"What about something that belongs to the witch?" Ella asks. "Is there anything of hers that was left here?"

"There was this bag," Ashley holds up a small back-pack. Brohn squints, inspecting it as Ella grabs it.

"This will do." Ella whistles and then throws a small acorn on the ground. A sudden explosion, a puff of smoke, then a roar. Standing in front of her as the smoke dissipates is a large and powerful looking hound.

"Did you just summon a beast?" Ashley asks.

"I did. Yes." Ella answers.

"You are a glitter blood?" The hunter puts her hand on her sword.

"Oh please. You hired us because we know how to work around the restrictions of the magecore. If I was a witch, why would I be helping you hunt a witch?"

"It's fine," Moses says, putting his hands up. "Ella

was trained by the magecore academy, she's always been eccentric, but her goal is to find the things that go bump in the night and put a sword through their hearts. You don't have to worry about her."

"That's high praise coming from Moses," Brohn adds. "He's not a fan of fey touched. Also, how are you gonna stand in all this viscera and be concerned about a cute puppy?"

Ashley squints and tilts her head. They watch her, as she looks at the hound. His big baleful eyes glisten, and his wet nose sniffs the air.

"Fine. Just warn me next time,"

"Perfect!" Ella puts the bag in the dog's face. "Give that a sniff, Philip."

"You named him Philip?" Brohn asks.

"You got a problem with that?"

"Nope. Just wondering, that's all."

"He's got a scent." Ella says as she moves out the door with Philip. "Let's go find a witch!"

Ella lectures as they move out of the city and into the northeastern territory outside Valeward. "Although it's called the Valeward Marshes, the reality of druidic conservational understanding of nature has defined an area of permanent fresh water saturation–that is to say an area that has seen a measurable amount of water for years or decades, that also has trees growing within it–as a swamp." The rest of the group continue to splash their way through the Valeward Marshes into a thicket of bushes and trees surrounded by small ponds and streams.

"Obviously, you can see the trees around us, so in all respects the Valeward Marshes should be called the Valeward Swamps," Ella continues.

"It doesn't matter what it's called, Ella," Moses says. "We're here to look for a witch, Remember? Maybe stop announcing our arrival like a weirdo."

"I'm just saying this is a swamp, not a marsh, so we need to be aware of things that hunt in swamps."

"Like witches?" Brohn asks. "Can I just mention again how out of my comfort zone we are. I got put in charge of the bar earlier, which stressed me out. Now I'm hunting a witch that blew two people up."

"You're a valuable member of the guild, Brohn," Moses says.

"Yeah, for keeping peace in the Penny Lich. What am I supposed to do out here?" Brohn opens his large wingspan and gestures to the whole marsh, er, swamp. "Punch a witch in the face with my bare fists?"

"I don't think they're resistant to bludgeoning damage," Ashley says. "So, punch away." The hound that Ella summoned stops at a collection of aspen trees, leafless and dark against the foggy evening sky. "I think your demon hound has found something, Elderberry."

"Your name is Elderberry?" Brohn asks.

"It's Ella," Ella says, then turns to Ashely. "And it's not a demon hound, it is just a hound, summoned from Faerie."

"The fey lands?" Moses asks. Stepping through a puddle. "So that's a fey dog?"

Brohn's head jerks up. "When he's happy he wags his fairy-tail."

"It doesn't matter," Ashley says. "Your hound is pointing to something."

"Then I suppose we should check it out."

As the party comes around the tree line, the smell hits Brohn first while the others begin to investigate.

Seemingly unaffected by the stench, Ashley, Moses and Ella move toward the source, while Brohn covers his mouth and gags. They find a clump of rotting cloth and extra bits.

"Can you please act like you smell this too?" Brohn asks.

"It's a kill," Ella says.

"A peasant from town," Moses says

"Another victim of the witch," Ashley pushes.

"No," Moses says looking at the pile of bloody rags left on the ground. A smoking fire pit shows that someone was camping, but all other evidence only points to murder.

"This body is nothing like those in the hut." Moses points out the crimson streaks moving away from the site.

"This is something else," Ella says, touching the blood and looking at the rags. "Something killed the person here, then dragged the body away." She moves quickly, preparing her bow. Like the fiery red hair that trails behind her, the rest of the group follows.

"A bear?" Brohn asks as he catches up to her.

Her eyes are on the ground. "No. It would have eaten the body there. No beast. This is a monster." She purses her lips and lets air fill her cheeks, then presses it out and does this several times, making the sound of a bird in the trees. Philip comes to her side, then together they jump around the bush.

The party sees a middle aged man crying at the side of a pond.

Brohn and Moses both lighten their glares, but Ashley and Ella both stay vigilant.

"Sir?" Moses asks. "Are you ok?"

"What do you think you're doing?" Ashley hisses, pulling him back.

"The man needs help," Moses says. "He could be hurt or have just lost someone."

"Or he could be a werewolf." Ashley says.

"Or a vampire," Ella continues, "A ghost, a ghoul, a corrupted elf, oblex, doppelganger, changeling, di-morphic change–"

"Ok. I get it, it's dangerous," Moses says. "But this is what I have to do. This is my job." He walks toward the crying man "Plus, you guys are just paranoid. You always look for the worst in people." He gets closer. "Sir, I'm a paladin of the Valeward Kingdom. I work with the Temple of The Hallowed Conclave. And sir, while I am technically employed by them, and through them the magecore, I must make it known, sir...that I am actually a hired contractor. I represent them through the power of the Penny Lich Guild. Now sir, I will say that we originally called ourselves the People's Guild, but realized that since our headquarters was the Penny Lich tavern, we would just stick with that. Sir? Do you understand? Sir? It's a branding issue, see the People's Guild is very open ended, but the Penny Lich Guild gives us more of an identity. Sir? Sir?"

"He gets it, Moses," Ella says. "Move on."

By this time Moses has made his way near the man. As the quiet of the Valeward Marshes sets in, the lap-ping of the pond, the gentle breeze in the leaves, a new sound begins to rise.

"Sir, are you growling right now?"

The rumbling from the man's throat deepens and grows louder.

"Sir, I'm gonna have to ask you to stop, uh, growl-ing, if you'd like us to help you." Moses begins to step back. But as he does, a small twig snaps under his foot.

The man's head snaps toward Moses. Hollow eyes

drip with black goo, and dark blood covers his mouth. Moses quickly turns back to the party.

"I've made a terrible mista–" before Moses can finish the sentence, the lengthy purplish figure of the man glides through the air and wraps around Mose's body.

"Horrible mistake!" Moses says. The creature lifts its head back, black teeth exposed from a wide open mouth. "Hey, sir!" Moses struggles to throw the body off him. "You better put those teeth back where they belong!"

"You can't let it bite you!" Ella says, aiming her crossbow, "It's a Velki."

"You know this creature?" Ashley asks.

"I know of them. They are corrupted elves from the north. It's said that the fungal forests to the north corrupts the high elves. Corrupted elves are cast out from their crystal cities to wander the world–"

"Ella! For Divine's sake, shut up and shoot!" Moses shouts. "Hey, no biting! No chomping down, dude! I'm soup!"

"Hold still," Ella says. Moses stops and looks back to see the blacked fangs descending down on his neck. Then the creature lets go of his body. A hole appears in his head and the bolt from Ella's crossbow flies into the swamp.

Moses slides his hands over his body in disgust. "Get off of me, ya elven bitch! That's right, you come for the feast but you get the fists!" He throws his hands up in a fighting stance.

The creature begins to move, stretching out toward Moses. The Paladin yelps and jumps back toward the party. Together they watch as the corrupted elf begins to stand back up.

"So much help you were back there," Moses says to

Brohn as they back away.

"What do you want me to do, Moses? Punch the zombie swamp elf? No thank you." Brohn says.

"Why is it getting back up?" Ashley asks, getting her sword ready.

"It's infected with the same gloomdew that corrupts parts of the fungal forest."

"So?" Ashley demands.

"So," Ella says, readying her shot. "That creature isn't an elf anymore. It's a husk, a corpse. It's being driven by the gloomdew."

"So there's no killing it?" Brohn asks.

"I didn't say that." Ella watches the creature stumble closer to them. They all prepare for the encounter. "Though everyone who tried to kill one ended up as one."

"This is a waste of our time," Ashley says. "We need to find that little witch, and take care of her."

"Little?" Ella asks. Then Ashley pulls a strand of her blond hair from her head, and begins tying a loop into each end. Black ichor pours from the Veiki's mouth, and its bones crack as it walks.

Ashley slips the loops onto her pointer and middle finger.

Ella, Brohn, and Moses step back as the creature stumbles closer.

It looms large in Ashley's view. She speaks ritual words and forces her fingers apart, ripping the hair into two.

Just as the creature is bearing down on her, its fleshy decay preparing to wrap around her, the hair snaps. The corrupted elf vanishes with a sudden pop. Ashley begins to stumble, and her legs grow weak.

Moses jumps forward and grabs her before she falls, his face filled with wonder and awe. "What did you do?" He asks.

"Oh, just a little banishment spell," She says weakly.

"You gotta teach me that one," Ella says beaming with excitement.

"You ok?" Moses asks Ashley.

"Yeah, it just takes a bit out of me, that's all." Ashley smiles.

"Well, next time. Give me a little warning, eh?" Moses chuckles and pulls her up straight.

The house they find in the swamps of Valeward certainly looks like it holds a witch. Arching black trees lower willow-like tendrils around the shack. A torch lights the door to the creaky, old wooden structure as the night begins to take over the sky.

"So, this is one hundo percent a hag's house, right?" Brohn asks as the party looks over a group of bushes.

"It's just a fishing shack," Ella says, petting her hound. He licks her, and she gives him a small treat.

"But your dog brought us here, and we're looking for a witch."

"Witches and hags are different," Ella says.

"Hags are creatures that come from the shadow realm. Witches are a group of women that study arcane magic outside of the laws of the magecore."

"Oh, kinda like you?" Brohn says to Ella. Ella shoots him a pointed look, then at Ashely who is focused on the house.

"No," Ella says calmly. "Everything I know, I learned from the magecore academy."

"Yeah, I know some stuff too, ya know," Moses says, looking over his sword. "Magic, I mean. Yeah, Elliot, he's like a cleric wizard genius, he taught me how to do some cool stuff."

Ashley turns and replies, "Oh yeah? Like what?"

"Uh, you know. Just some simple stuff, like presdi-digitationon." Moses says as Ashley smirks. "Maybe, later, you could teach me that, uh, that banishment spell?"

"Oh, you wanna get rid of me that much?" Ashley says playfully.

"What? No!"

A glass breaks in the hut, and the party's attention turns. Moses and Ashley ready their blades, Ella aims her crossbow, and Brohn holds up his fists.

Moses says, "I'll go first. Brohn, you cover me, and Ashely you bring up the rear. Ella, you keep an eye out and shoot anything that tries to run."

Within several seconds the team moves up to the house. Moses puts his back against the wall at the entryway, Brohn hits the opposite side, flanking the old door. Moses peeks through the window and sees a figure sitting at a table. It has long stringy hair and torn up clothing.

Moses moves his fingers toward the door, and Brohn moves in, while Ashley takes his spot on the wall. Brohn moves his large frame and kicks the door open with barely an effort. Moses spins and moves into the room.

They proceed quickly and fill the small hut, surrounding the witch at the table. A well used candle lights a broken plate in front of her. She moves her hand trying to meld the pieces of ceramic back together. While the parts fuse, they leave large janky scars from their break.

The witch looks up from her practice and catches the party off guard with large tearful eyes and quivering lips. Freckles cover her face, and she looks thin, tired, and hungry.

"Hallowed Conclave," Moses says. "She's no older than ten years old."

The basement cellar of the Penny Lich:

"I mean, she's not gonna blow me up if I'm bringing her some cheese, right?" Brohn says, standing at the door. Ella continues to etch runes on the wood which glow with soft magic.

"I don't know, Brohn," she says. "She seemed peaceful when we found her, and she was asleep the entire trip back."

"True," Brohn says, going for the door knob.

"Unless, she was only pretending to be asleep," Ella goes on, "so she could find our base of operations, and then destroy us from within? A bloody and fiery end to us all, melting our skin and boiling our organs in our own blood." Her eyes wide while staring at the runes on the door. Brohn's lips quiver, eyes unblinking. Then Ella relaxes and continues to etch her magic. "Or maybe she's just a kid and some weird stuff happened to her." She shrugs her shoulders.

Brohn looks between Ella and the door. His mouth opens and closes several times as he croaks out unspoken words.

"Wha... I uh, but..."

"Either way, if she gets too hungry, she might not like it," Ella says, twisting the door knob and cracking open the door.

The thin line of light from outside the cellar door widens in the room as the door swings in. Standing in the light of the world, Brohn holds a tray and shivers.

"I brought cheese," he says in shaken words.

He takes a step into the basement. Lit by torches that cast as many shadows as they extinguish, the room reminds Brohn of the basement with the troll.

His teeth rattle at the memory. His steps are slow and deliberate.

"There's a nice farmer's cheese here," he stammers, holding the plate of food out. "Which obviously was just cottage cheese that we let sit out too long, but you know, roll that on some bread and bam you have a... you have a, uh..." He smacks his dry lips, "Uh, less horrible meal."

"Leave me alone." A voice whispers throughout the room.

Brohn stops, stiffens, and looks around. "Ok, obviously you're awake, and probably not sure where you are. And while we have you imprisoned here in our basement, I want you to know, tha--"

"A prisoner? You think I'm a prisoner?" The whispers come from behind him. Brohn turns to the door, and a dark figure wisps past. He drops the plate with a slight yelp.

"Ok, I'll level with you, I'm not a fan of basements. Kay? Last time I got in a fight with a troll and I have a thing in my back now. You know, like in my lower left side? I can stretch it and stuff, but it always feels—"

"If I wanted to leave, I would," the whisper says, as it rounds out into a little girl's voice. Brohn watches as the shadow stands in the doorway and drops away, revealing the girl. Her pale skin reflects what little light comes from the door. Her hair is braided and dirty, her clothes ragged.

"What's your name?" Brohn asks.

"This place, can I stay here?" The girl asks.

"I mean, we have some rooms upstairs. Ella stays in one of the rooms, maybe you can room with her."

"Absolutely not." Ella says as she pulls a hand crossbow out.

"Is that to kill me with?"

"If I wanted you dead--"

"Hey." Brohn stops Ella. "Child." He nods at the girl.

"Witch," Ella says.

"You're not going to help me, are you?" the girl spits. "You just want to kill me."

"No," Brohn says.

"Maybe. Are you going to try and blow us up?" Ella asks.

"Like my parents?"

"Those were your parents?" Brohn steps forward. The girl takes her eyes from Ella to Brohn, then down at the ground and looks at her hands. Tears begin dripping on to the ground.

"I...I'm so sorry. I didn't mean to. My mommy was right, I'm an abhorrent." Her eyes begin to glow in darkness. "They were so angry, and I was so tired of the belt."

"Hey, it's ok," Brohn says, getting closer. The girl backs away again, but this time knocks into Ella.

"Please don't hurt me!" she screams as a black fluid spews from her mouth. Her feet lift up off the ground, and she reacts to painful slaps to her body. "Daddy, please. Please I promise I didn't do magic."

"No, no, girl, please." Brohn moves forward and grabs the girl's arm. She turns now looking down on him and anger and pain flow through her. She screams, Ella aims her crossbow for the girl's head.

"You need to control it, Girl," Ella says. "I don't want to hurt you."

"Hurt me?"

"Probably shouldn't have said that." Brohn sees a black mass of inky magic form from her hands. It gathers and swings toward him, knocking him back.

"Divine damn it," Ella says. She pulls the trigger, but

the bolt holds still. A dark hand forms around the bolt and holds it in place. Ella quickly throws the crossbow, and pulls out a gem, speaking an incantation.

The girl pushes past Ella and floats up into the main floor of the tavern. As she makes her way out, the door begins to close. Ella at the last moment jumps out of the basement and watches as the door locks.

"Ella!?" Brohn shouts from in the basement.

"Uh, yeah, Brohn?"

"Am I stuck in here?"

"Uuuuh."

The sigil she finished on the door glows, as it fuses the door closed.

"Ella?" Brohn continues. "Did you finish the arcane lock?"

"Maybe."

"By maybe, do you mean yes, and now I'm magically sealed in here?'

"Maybe."

"And now there's a half crazed, shadow witch running amok in the tavern that Hadvar put me in charge of for one day."

"...Mmmmaybe. I believe in this situation, it's more logical that I go find Moses, and we stop her from doing more damage, which means I will have to leave you, Brohn." Ella looks up, hearing the screams of the patrons at the bar.

"Go, Ella. Sure, I have an aversion to basements. I mean, I was kept in basements almost my entire childhood, and I recently was almost murdered in one, but I can make it through this. I'm a grown man, I'm strong, I can do this. I can defeat the demons that live in my past. Like this little girl, I can overcome the shitty situation just like she has been given. I will overcome this, just as she can overcome her own demons and maybe, just maybe we can help her, you know? Find a way for her to live with the magic inside her. Penny Lich Guild for the win, right?"

Brohn stands at the magically sealed door, waiting for a response. "For the win, right? Ella?"

Silence.

"She totally heard all that," Brohn says to himself, looking for some farmer's cheese.

One of the Tavern rooms for rent:

Two beds are stuffed with feathers. Heavy plush blankets lay on the floor. A candle lights the room.

"I haven't been to such a nice Penny Lich Tavern since I stayed in Virgil," Ashley says as she gets her things packed.

"You've been to Virgil?"

"Indeed," she says. "My guild has deep roots in the west."

"How did you get into the hunting of witches? Crimson Tribunal?"

"The Crimson Tribunal is a guild that acts as a sort of accrediting organization for other hunter's guilds. Your Ella is registered with the Crimson Tribunal, but she seems to have found her own place."

"So you're both a part of the Crimson Tribunal, but you guys don't work for the same people?"

"Correct. I represent the Aberrant Hunters League. We are people who have been directly affected by the destruction that witches and hags bring to the world."

"You must do well for yourself here in Valeward."

"Not really, actually.In other parts of the world, we are a necessity, magic runs rampant and the governments do almost nothing to tamp it down. Here in Valeward, the magecore does that. We have almost no work to do here."

"Then what brought you here?" "Can I be real with you?" she asks.

"You can be so real," Moses leans in. "Reel it in, girl."

"I think you'll understand this, seeing as you're a paladin of the people, and you were fed up with the lack of magecore understanding."

"Oh yeah, that's me. We're like on the exact same page right now," Moses says.

"I came here because of you," Ashley says. Moses stops, face frozen, eyebrows cocked.

"You came here because of me?"

"Yeah. Word has spread through Yonder Valley of the Penny Lich Guild. The paladin that saw the magecore lacking and did something about it. It's inspirational. And I had to come meet you."

Visibly upset, Moses backs away. He turns to walk to the door.

"Is it so weird?" Ashley asks. "You're a paladin. Your kind are trained to seek glory. The name of the paladin is their legacy, is it really so odd that people talk about you trying to do something great?"

"Yeah, Ashley, I think it is." He leans on the door frame now, thinking. "I didn't become a paladin for the glory."

"Why did you?" She steps closer.

"The money," Mose smirks again. She shoves him softly. "No, I was just a temple guard. And then I got chosen for a church supply run to the Harrowing Coast. I must have impressed someone along the way, and they inducted me."

Ashley studies him. "Seems like you regret that."

"I don't."

"Mmhmm. You could have left the training at any time. If you didn't want to be one, then why put yourself through the challenges."

Moses chews on his lip as memories pass over his eyes. When he starts talking it's slow and calculated. "They chose me because of this," he points to his eyes. "People expect something from me because of my blood. I know that."

"The Mythbood?" She says, touching the side of his face. "Your eyes."

"Despite being thought of as perfect, I'm fallible. I've made mistakes, big ones." He watches her eyes. She seems attentive, caring. She almost seems accepting. "And I used the paladin status as a way to hide from my mistakes. Then I realized that I can use the title to make up for them. Maybe."

"You don't seek the glory of your god, or king, or yourself.You seek redemption. It's honorable. Truly."

"Thank you. What about you? Why did you become a witch hunter?"

She swings her hips back and forth, pushing her hands behind her. ""When I was a child my parents were killed by a witch. I swore vengeance. The Aberrant Hunters League took me in and taught me how to make that happen."

"That's a sad story."

"It's literally the same story we all have. We are a walking cliche."

"Wow, I never, yeah I guess."

"But that's the problem. It's not original, sure, but it's real. Magic runs wild in the world and someone needs to do the job that the kingdoms of Onto won't. Even the magecore here in Valeward didn't care enough for the grindstone commoners to investigate the murder of those people. But you inspired me to."

He takes her hands and holds them on his chest, a smile cracks on her face. The intense focus of a hunter beams from her eyes. "You know what else I found in Virgil?"

Moses leans in. "Tell me." He closes his eyes,

"Paladins who are not sworn to celibacy, but let their passion for righteousness bleed into nightly conquests." She leans in, their lips close to giving into their passions, when a scream comes from below. There is a thudding and footsteps pound toward them. Suddenly, and before Moses can pull away fully, Ella is at the door of the room.

"Hey, guys," she says. "I think we have a situation."

Moses runs down the stairs, as the two women jump from the second floor balcony and land with their weapons posed. Both have swords at the ready, the witch in their sights.

"Ok," Moses says, annoyed as he comes off the stairs. "Was that necessary? She's already scared off all the patrons."

"Sorry to show you up by being prepared," Ella says. Moses pulls out his sword, and it crackles with divine energy.

"We need to take her out as soon as we can," Ashley says. "She is a witch of the shadow, which means she can summon–"

The girl floats in the air near the fireplace, her hands and feet covered in ashy smoke. She twitches as magic flows through her, and she holds out her hand. Several tables are set ablaze and several more are covered in a dark substance.

The girl pulls her hand up, and from the darkness of the fireplace an ashy shadow hound growls and steps forward. Several of the black ooze like piles begin to giggle and warp into human-like forms.

"--shadow creatures to fight for her," Ashley finishes.

Initiative falls into place and the first round of battle begins. The shadow dog runs forward and attacks Moses. The two sludgemen both quickly swing for the ladies.

Moses feels the teeth of the hound sink into his arm and throws it across the room, charging it quickly with his blazing sword. The two clash near the bar.

A sludgeman swipes at Ella, but she dodges the attack, spins around and puts her sword into the creature's back. It holds her blade and spins around.

"Ah, a shadowspawn," Ella says. "Let's see how you like this." Ella throws her hand forward and a beam of light releases from it. The shadow creature recoils and lets go of her blade.

Ashley pulls out her second blade and holds off the claws that the shadow sludge created to slice her. She finds her ground enough to push it back. It throws its claws out and screams. The sound fills her ears and she can feel a terror in her soul begin to rise up. She is fighting a creature from another dimension of existence. Something that lives only to consume the life of everything around it. She couldn't help but feel the fluttering fear of death in her heart.

Ashley remembers that she is a creature of death as well. She was a force of nature, she would never run from such a creature, she delighted in its death, she let her blade loose on them

Quickly, Ashley runs forward and slices the creature with her two swords. A blue magic inlay glows as the blades break the darkness of the creature's body apart. She slides as the shadow jumps for her and then brings the shadow creature down with her magic blades.

Moses grabs the locket around his neck and whispers a prayer as the darkness of a creature surrounds him. It begins to envelop his glowing bright sword and bronze armor, when suddenly the sword moves quickly upward and slashes through the creature. The sludge-like monster sizzles and screams in pain as it dissipates.

Ashley turns to the witch and shoots a bolt, hitting her in the arm. The girl screams and the blood pouring from the wound turns black and floats in the air around her. Ashley pulls a new bolt out and aims it. As she pulls the trigger, Ella kills the sludge monster, and throws a dagger, hitting Ashley's crossbow.

"You can't kill her," Ella says.

"She's a witch! What else did you think I was going to do with her?" Ashley asks as she grabs another bolt.

A pounding resounds from the basement, and the sound of footsteps can be heard ascending the stairs. "I... guys, I did it, I finally overcame my own fears and insecurities and was able to defeat my own demons. I'm coming!"

Seeing the fight between Ella and Ashley, Moses plucks one of his hairs from his head and begins to tie it around his fingers, chanting the words of the banishment ritual as he remembered it. He aims the spell for the floating witch near the fireplace. She seizures and shakes in the air as black tentacles form around her.

"Moses, no!" Ella runs toward the paladin, but Ashley turns her aim to the girl again.

"How's it going for you guys?" Brohn asks as he arrives in the tavern. Ashley is preparing to shoot the witch, who has black tendrils forming out of her blood, eyes blackened and body pale and shaking. Ella spins around to put a blade to Ashley while Moses finishes his ritual.

In a supernatural burst of speed, Brohn moves past the others and jumps between the witch and Ashley's bolt. He had done this a thousand times as a child. It was a party trick to make quick buck. Catch the bolt. Let it sail past his body and catch it.

He leaps in the air as the missile flies. The witch behind him, he sails through the air, ready to catch the thing, but feels an odd cold sliver on his back. One of her tentacles rubs him and sends a chill through his body. He's thrown off for a microsecond, and the crossbow bolt stops in his hand.

Literally in his hand. He looks at the projectile as it sinks its way through the flesh of his palm and breaks through the back of it. As he screams in pain, the girl looks down at him and catches him with her tendrils. And Moses finishes his spell.

With a sudden pop, the witch holding Brohn vanishes from existence. The room is suddenly and deafeningly quiet. Moses throws his hands in the air and shouts.

"Hollowed Conclave, yes! That's Divine Blessed right, Fungal Monkey!" He celebrates while both Ashley and Ella stare at him in disbelief. "Woo! I banished you. That's right, I learned a new spell and it worked."

"You banished Brohn!" Ella says. "You banished a little girl."

"It's fine," Ashley says, getting her crossbow ready. "The spell only lasts a minute or so. That gives us time to prep and kill her when she reappears."

"No," Ella says. "I won't let you kill that girl."

"She's a witch, Ella. You of all people should know what she's capable of."

"I do. Which is why I won't let you kill her. There are people in the world that can help her."

"The world is better off if she doesn't exist, that's

what the Aberrant Hunters League does: we kill
witches. She killed those people."

"Her parents," Ella retorts.

"All the more reason.She has no sympathy for us
normal people. She'll kill us all."

"Normal? You think we're normal? Look at what we
just did. What I can do. Who's your next target?"

"That's not how we work. Moses gets it." Ashley
walks over to him, putting her hand on his shoulder.
"We are what it takes to make the world better."

"Is that true, Moses?" Ella asks. "Are you going to
help her murder this little girl?"

Moses looks between them. Every second he can feel
the spell wearing away and the banishment preparing
to release.

"It's not that I want to murder a little girl," Moses
starts. Ella rolls her eyes, "It's just I don't want to be
stuck between you two. You know. It's kinda awkward."

"Moses," Ashley says, "Please tell me you understand what we can accomplish together, what I came
all the way here for. I came here to find and help you.
Let's do this together."

Ella looks at the ground, her eyes unable to meet
theirs and she remembers the feeling of dread that
came with marrying Elliot, the uncertainty, the feeling
that she's doing the wrong thing. She then looks up
and sees Moses staring into Ashley's eyes.

"Moses," Ella says, "You cannot let this happen. I
know that we've never seen eye to eye, but you can't
do this. We're talking about the life of a child. I know
that somewhere deep below your armor you have a
heart that can see that this is evil. For the sake of the
Divine, please don't do this." Tears form in Ella's eyes.

Moses looks at her for a moment and breaths in. He

clicks his tongue and grabs Ashley's hand. Looking down at her, he winks and says, "I think it would be more efficient if you got the rest of the Hunters for this. It seems like a powerful wild magic witch."

Ella lets the tear fall from eyes and shakes with sadness and anger.

"You should hurry. I can only hold this spell for so long," Moses says.

"You're so right. Of course," Ashley says. She turns to Ella and sees the anger rising, "Do you want me to take care of her?"

"No, I got her. You go. Hurry back. I don't want you to miss the fun." Moses pushes her toward the door and she chuckles and runs.

Ella opens her eyes in time to see Moses watch Ashely leave. He waves her out and turns back with a dopey smile. Ella prepares herself, not for the fight or for how to murder Moses, but for the conversation she'll have with Elliot to explain it all. He'll be upset, undoubtedly, but she can convince him that it was the right thing to do.

"Hey Elliot, you know your old friend Moses, turns out he's a child murdering monster and I had to put him down," she thinks in her head as she contemplates which dagger she's going to use to slit Moses' throat. "But it's ok, cause I found this random homeless guy on the street who I think would be a better replac–"

Her thought is interrupted by Moses dropping his sword and his smile fading. She begins to register what his face means when he begins to speak. "Ella you have to help me." Moses gets on his knees. "That chick is insane, and she's obsessed with me. I need your help to get rid of her!"

The Ether:

The expansive and unknowable realm of the ether tethers all places together. It is the space between all things. It is a place where nightmares come to rest, and darkness dwells as the sun brightens the world. It is a place to be sailed only by the greatest of wizards and gods. It is a place where Brohn screams as the witch holds him with her dark tendrils.

Brohn looks around to see the girl falling unconscious, her shadow magic fading.

"Hey, hey, girl," he says as he rights himself. He feels his body move without needing to physically move itself. Instead it feels like a dream. Quickly breaking the bolt and pulling it from his hand, he flinches but moves closer to the girl. Grabbing her hand, her eyes clear. "What's your name?"

With the last moment of consciousness the girl smiles and says, "Olive."

The Penny Lich Tavern:

"You banished them," Ella says matter of factly, but expecting an answer.

"Listen, I wanted to keep Ashley from killing her."

"Why?" She begins making her way up to the second floor, to the rooms for rent.

"You said it yourself, she's a child, just a little girl."

"What is she to you? A girl that blew up her parents and tore up the Penny Lich, right? Elliot's gonna kill you for that one by the way."

"We have to survive the Aberrant Hunters League first," Moses says, grabbing Ella's hand as they get to the top of the staircase. "Hey, Ella. I'm sorry."

"What are you sorry for?"

Moses sucks air in through his teeth and squirms.

"You don't even know what I'm upset about do you?"

"I mean, I can guess so many things," Moses says. She turns her head and lifts an eyebrow. "Is it because I didn't change the toilet parchment?"

She huffs and walks away.

"Listen, Ella, I need your help. OK?" Moses says running around to get in front of her. "I'm sorry for whatever I did, but I have a plan to help this girl, and I need you."

"You only need me cause you bamfed the only other person who would be willing to help you."

"That's not true."

"It is. And you think that I should feel honored to help you, right? A fey touched like me? I should be just so happy that the great and holy Moses Summerhill would look upon me with use. To see past my 'disability.' To want to use me."

"Is that what this is about?" Moses says.

"Moses, are you serious?" Ella looks him directly in the eyes with accusation. He thinks for a moment about the last time she looked him in the eyes. He shivers in the truth. She never had. "You don't even remember saying it earlier do you? I'm just here for the weirdos and freaks. You think so highly of yourself, that when you kill and muderer its for a greater good. But when I do it, it's because I'm messed up in the head, right? I fight monsters, Paladin Moses, I fight the things that would eat your terror like it was a broth, and finish you off by crunching your bones. I help people, same as you, but because I'm different, you blow it off. I fight every, single, monster I find. You and Elliot are so afraid of what I do that you've made that into something twisted, and maybe it is, but at the end of the day I do it because I want to help the world," She points to the front door, "I want to help people like that girl.

"I know that, Ella, that's why I want your help to fix this," Moses argues.

"You don't get it do you? I have spent years fighting. I have spent my life learning about this. Witches, Glitterbloods, Aberrations. I have done this, time and time again. This isn't the first time I've dealt with the Aberrant Hunters League. But you don't even stop to ask what I would do. You don't care what I think. You look at me as some lower entity that you need to lead around on a leash. Some child that you need to watch over."

"Ella, I have a plan, and I really care abou–" Moses says, reaching forward without thinking. She knocks his hands away. She can see his emotion, she assumes its sadness or concern.

"Don't tell me you care, Moses." Her voice shakes. "You've spent years belittling me because of who I am and what I do. You made Elliot choose between us, and you've made me feel like a freak from the moment we met. I thought I could do this, I thought I could help Elliot with what's coming, but I can't."

"Wait, what's coming?"

"You wouldn't believe me, even if I told you. Cause I'm just some stupid fey touched freak, excused me, I have to pack before your spell wares off," she says as she pushes past him and into the room where she's been staying.

Moses stands in shock of the encounter he just had. His mind reels in the memories of all the times he spoke to her, to the friendship he built with Elliot at the devastation of Elliot's childhood with Ella. He thought about his being at their wedding, but his vocal concerns with it. Thinking through the pain he never saw in her eyes as he called her out for being weird and untrustworthy. How he was filled with dread at the sight of her. He clicks his tongue and bites his lip. His eyes grow large in revelation as he nods.

"Does nobody pay for a room in this place?"

The Ether:

"Hey, Olive," Brohn says. "Olive, wake up."

The girl begins to stir in her sleep. She opens her eyes and sees Brohn floating over her. She reacts with a blast of magical energy. Brohn takes the hit on his forearms.

"No, wait," he says.

"What have you done with me?" The girl asks. She looks around. "Where am I?"

"We...where are we?" He corrects.

"What have you done with me?"

"I was kinda hoping you could tell me," Brohn says, as they float in the nothingness of the void. Wafting smoke passes them every once in a while, and distant lights flicker in the dark.

"Why would I know?" the girl asks.

"Cause you're all..." He cricks his neck and puts his fingers out in odd directions. "... you're a, you know."

"An Abhorrent."

"A what? Do you mean an aberrant?

"No, my daddy, he called me abhorrent." Her face twists in sadness. "Before I killed him and mommy."

"Hey, hey, hold on," Brohn says. The girl continues to cry. "Eh, Uh, here!" He pulls something out of his pocket. The girl looks down and sees a colorful shiny ball in Brohn's palm.

She stops crying, "What's that?"

"What's this?" He responds, unwrapping the ball from the clear wrapping. It slips out from his grip and begins floating away. "Oh, catch that!" He points at it.

The girl quickly moves forward and grabs the ball, taking more notice of it.

"That, in your hand is a jawrock. You put it in your mouth and suck on it."

"Why?"

"Go ahead, it's for you," he offers. She's about to pop it in her mouth when she gets a suspicious look on her face.

"How long has this been in your pants?" she asks.

"Not that long. Two or three days tops."

"Days?!"

"It was in the wrap. It's fine. Just try it, what else have you got going on?"

She thinks it through and then pops the ball in her mouth. She swishes it around and waits for something to hap–

"It's so good!" She squeals. The sweet flavors combine with a soft sour that makes her mouth salivate and crave more.

"They're my favorite. When I was your age, I would go between families a lot. I was used for other people's benefit. They would make me hurt people so they could make money. And sometimes when I did a really good job, I would earn a jawrock."

"You had to hurt people for this?"

"I used to. I was really good at it, but I learned to stand up for myself, and now I help protect people."

"So you still hurt people, but you get to choose who you hurt?"

He looks off in concerned thought. "Well, yeah, I guess that's the sum of it." He shakes his distant stare. "And every once in a while I want to remind myself about the sweet things in the hard times. I hated my families, but I really liked jawrocks." He pulls out a second one and unwraps it. "Like a lot."

It shoots forward the same as the last, and he begins to fly forward toward it. As he gets closer, his wounded hand reaching out to grasp it, the jawrock slips into a nothingness in the ether and disappears. Still moving forward, Brohn watches as his own hand slips out of sight, and he does everything he can to stop himself.

"OLIVE!!!" he screams in a high pitched voice. "Olive, help me with your voodoo!"

Olive turns to see him beginning to disappear, and she reacts with her eyes turning dark and tendrils warping out of her body.

"Olive, I gave you candy. You owe me," he screams.

"I don't want to hurt you," she says.

"Better than getting sucked into an ether void butthole. Help me," he yells as his whole arm is consumed in the nothingness of the hole, and his head begins to disappear.

"Mr. Brohn, I can't"

"It's just Brohn, and I really believe in you, and not 'cause you're my only hope of escaping this terrifying situation, I also think you're a strong and marvelous little g–" His head fully disappears.

Olive squirms, then shoots her tentacles. The first one flies forward and stops quickly as it slaps Brohn on the butt. A muffled anger shifts through his body. The second tentacle grabs his ankle and begins pulling him back.

Olive then grasps with the first and the third tentacles. As she starts to pull him back she realizes that she has nothing to prop herself on and feels herself moving forward. As soon as Brohn's body gets halfway enveloped in the void hole, he slips through quickly and pulls her forward. Before she knows what's happening she is being pulled through the space that exists outside of the ether.

Ella's room at the Penny Lich (which she has yet to pay for):

Ella stuffs her clothes into a leather sack and counts several things, mumbling reminders to herself.

"Knock knock," Moses says.

"You do that on purpose don't you?" Ella asks, focusing on her work.

"Yeah, I started doing it as a joke to mess with Elliot, and now it just kinda happens."

"Sounds about right."

"Listen, uh," Moses looks around and finds a spot on a bed to sit. He tries to cross his legs, but his armor makes it difficult, and he gives up. "I'm sorry about earlier, I should have heard you out before I started taking over."

"That's true," Ella says.

"Right, and uh, I would be happy to be a part of the plan you have going on. I don't want to get in your way, I want to help."

"Ok," Ella continues to pack.

"Ok?" Moses says tentatively.

"Yeah."

"Alright."

A moment passes, Moses stands up awkwardly. He opens his mouth, points his finger out, then stops. Closes his mouth, curls his finger back in. Then walks toward the door. Stops, turns. Then grimaces as he speaks, "It just... It seems like, maybe it's not alright?"

Ella stops packing for a moment, then continues folding clothes.

Moses pushes, "Listen, I'm so–"

"That," Ella says.

"What?" Moses asks.

"You say 'listen', so much, Moses," Ella begins. "Do you have any idea how pompous that sounds? Like every sentence, every word you have to say is so important that you need to make sure everyone hears it? And I know you say it to me because you think I'm not listening, not paying enough attention to you. You think because I'm fey touched that I'm more susceptible to infringing on your right of speech."

"Ella, I don't--"

"Dude, shut up." Ella looks at him directly, and the dread fills Moses again. "For once in your gifted life, shut up and listen."

He shuts his mouth, she turns her head and thinks for a moment and then continues, "Since the moment you came into Elliot's life, you've made him better. I saw that. You gave him strength, and he would have never gotten out of the Candle Crypts without you. I see you. It's one of the reasons I left; I knew that Elliot was better off in your hands than mine. I just want you to see me for what I can offer, too."

"Ella, I don't know what you want from me," Moses says. "I apologized, I came here to make it right."

"Did you? Did you really?"

"Yes. See me standing here? That's how it works," he points to the outside of the door and jumps out of the room. "Not apologetic." He jumps back in the room. "Apologetic."

He jumps out. "Hard hearted and stubborn." He jumps back in. "Groveling on my knees for mercy."

Ella watches him for a moment, her eyes overflowing with emotion. "You have spent years making fun of me, calling me names, and ostracizing me.And now, I'm just supposed to forgive you? You're nice to me for half a day, and then you call me weird when I have a plan, and I'm supposed to be the bigger person? How can you expect me to let you in like that, Moses? You're a paladin of the magecore. You suppress magic and bully weirdos like me. You're my enemy."

The words hang in the air.

Moses opens a section of his armor, unstrapping leather and unhinging plates. He then pulls out a small piece of leather. Carefully, he opens the loose wallet folds and hands a small hand sized parchment to Ella.

"What's this?" Ella asks.

"This is the reason I'm a paladin. This is the reason I continue on everyday. This is my mistake and my reason to live."

Ella looks up at him. She turns her head in question.

Moses continues, "If you can find it in your heart to forgive me, I swear to you Ella, I will do better. And I will let you in, if you let me in. If you want, I think we can still be friends."

"Does Elliot know about—"

"No one knows," Moses says sternly. "Except you."

Ella folds the parchment up, and hands it back. "I understand," she says. Her eyes calculate. Her tongue clicks, and she squints her eyes. "I can let you help."

"Really? Just like that?"

"If I now know your secret, then I get it, and we will have something to talk about when I return."

"When you return?"

"Yes. That little girl could learn to be one of the greatest mages our generation has ever seen, or she could become the monster that Ashley is looking for. We need to find the right people to help her. I know of an academy to the west, on Ammorith Hook. She and I will leave for the Wild Knoll Wood. I'll take her to the academy, and you get rid of me for a while. Everyone wins, except for Ashley."

"That's a pretty solid plan, actually." Moses says.

"And look at that, a fey touched can actually do something right," Ella says sharply.

"I get it, I'm an ass." Moses looks away in shame, but then his face changes to stern and focused. "Now let's go save a witch," he says, putting the leather back. He then starts to get his armor strapped together again, fumbling a bit. The latch on the plate armor doesn't quite fit. "Hold on on sec," he says, fidgeting with the latch, "just gotta get..."

"Do you need hel–"

"No! Nope," Moses lashes out, then chuckles. "No I got this." He goes for another latch and gets it done. He breathes out, runs his hand over his hair and smolders. "let's go save a witch."

Through the hole in the Ether:

Blackness, Brohn can say that all that exists is blackness. It always was, and always will be black. Forever and ever, black is the constant. The all consuming and unending, bound to be perceived, an eternity's width away.

Brohn knows that all things come from the black, and one day all things will return. The black is the space between the spaces. If the universe is a bubble, the Ether is the membrane that holds the universe together, and the black is the ocean that the bubble floats through.

His senses break apart like sugar in water, ever expanding until he has merged completely with the nothingness of the black, and he is no longer Brohn, but rather a piece of everything. Then as sugar crystalizes, he begins to cling to a form of creation that lingers outside of his understanding of time and space. He reconverges into Brohn within a realm, with his senses piecing together one at a time.

He feels the cool air, whipping past him. A scent of harvest wafts past him. His mind reels in the idea that he might be in the Threshing Moons month. It had just been Crown. Had he been gone that long. Sight eventually returns and he sees the world before him; it is sunset. An orange glow on the horizon fights the dark blue sky filled with dark clouds on the verge of breaking open with rain.

His body collects and he breathes hard. Falling, he hits a pumpkin and smashes it into juicy pieces. The moist soil grabs him and he lays still for a moment. Then he hears a screaming in the distance. It grabs his ear and pulls his attention. He looks but can't place it.

It circles around him, echoing and reverberating. Suddenly the screaming bursts and breaks through the air as black tendrils form where Brohn had just been standing. They slice the empty space and stretch nothingness to allow the screaming to come through. Then Olive begins to form between the two tentacles. Her body crystalized before Brohns eyes.

Her screaming stops as she becomes solid and fully formed. She then falls as Brohn did. He catches her and holds her low to the ground.

"I don't like void buttholes," she says weakly. "Where are we?"

"I don't know, Olive." Brohn looks behind him, and his stomach drops at the sight of something he can't comprehend. A great and gargantuan pyramid made of black glass overshadows him. The entirety of the structure, if such a small world can contain such a large piece of creation, is built so that the point of the pyramid balances on the ground, and the wide base of the thing looms hundreds, possibly thousands, of feet in the air.

The inverted pyramid reflects the orange light of the setting sun, and Brohn feels it looking down on him. He reaches his hand up in awe, wondering if this is a divine creature, if his mind is breaking at the sight of a thing that could never be. He catches himself, realizing that he stopped breathing in shock.

A voice snaps him from his upward gaze. He looks down and sees a figure approaching him. Long red hair, fiery in the setting sunlight, a wolf's fur cloak and a staff in her hand.

"How did you get here?" The voice demands. Behind her several glyphs spark in light, and Brohn looks past the woman at the light. "Where did you come from? Brohn," she says. "Brohn can you hear me? Where did you go?"

Brohn looks up at the woman approaching, he can see a green tattoo sleeve on the arm holding a staff, "How do you know my name, Greensleeve?"

"Brohn, it's me," the woman says. "Where did you go?"

Then a sudden pop resounds in Brohn's ears and wakes him from a stupor. The woman is gone, and in her place Ella stands over him and Olive.

"Ella?" Brohn blinks.

"Brohn, were you in the Ether? How long were you there?" Ella asks. "Did you see any Rithellians?"

"I saw, we saw," Brohn shakes his head in the memory. Like a dream, it slowly begins to fade from his mind. But something imprints on him, like a well worn stamp. The Pyramid, and the Greensleeve.

"Brohn, we gotta go," Ella says. "Before Ashely comes back with the Aberrant Hunters League."

"Sorry to tell you this," Moses says looking out a

window, "but they're already here."

The door to the Penny Lich opens and Ashley stands with weapons drawn, and several men in armor stand behind her.

The world is silent as the army of professional witch killers stands at the door of the Penny Lich. Ashley looks at Olive who is unconscious in Brohns arms. Watching long enough to see if her job is already done. She sees the girl still breathing, and her eyes narrow.

Within a split second Ashley moves toward the girl and slashes in the air for Olive's throat. Ella reacts, taking a dagger out in time to deflect the ambush. She grabs Olive and pulls her away from the attack, leaving Brohn behind at the end of Ashley's sword.

"I had a funny little feeling this was going to happen," Ashley says.

"You knew you were going to hold me at blade point?" Brohn says slowly standing up.

"Whoa there," Moses says. "What do you think is happening here, Ashley?"

"What do I think?" She turns her attention to Moses. " I think you've lost your way Paladin Moses. You left the church and the magecore to come work at a tavern."

"Well, I work from within a tavern. So, maybe get your facts straight."

"You flirt with women, despite your celibacy vows," she scolds.

"Hey, flirting isn't sex."

"It's temptation!"

"Are you saying I was tempting you?" Moses cocks an eyebrow.

"You can't stop yourself, can you?" Ella says, holding Olive and backing away from the other hunter.

"You're a traitor!" Ashely says. "I could sense something was wrong here, but I thought it was you the whole time." She points to Ella. "I figured you were corrupted by the darkness you hunt. But then, when we were in my room, I could still sense it in the air. And then you tried to kiss me."

"I didn't!" Moses says.

"You did what?" Brohn demands.

"I didn't!"

"He did. He closed his eyes and leaned in," Ashley says.

"I was just resting my eyes. It was dusty.... There was dust and a moth and...stuff."

"How did you do it?" Brohn asks.

"What?"

"How did you close your eyes?"

"I dunno," Moses says, "Like this?" He closes his eyes and leans in slightly.

"Oh COME ON!" Brohn yells and the other two groan. "That was a kiss."

"See? I told you." Ashley crossed her arms.

"No, it wasn't."

"Even I could tell, that was a kiss." Ella says.

"You're not helping."

"I'm not trying to."

"I thought we were friends now," Moses hisses.

"Are you going to try and kiss me if we are?" Ella quips.

"You pretend to be a righteous man," Ashley says, "But I can sense it, deep inside of you, you are not committed to your vow. You have abandoned your path, Moses. And I knew at that moment that I couldn't trust you."

"I mean, you're the one that brought up horny paladins from Virgil," Moses says, "Sounds like you wanted it as much as, er, I mean, uh. you wanted it, more... than... me."

Ashley narrows her eyes, "You work with shadow hunters, from a tavern, and now you aim to protect a witch. You are not the man I heard about, you are a liar and a fiend."

"Listen..." Moses begins, he stops and looks over to Ella, she smirks in a knowing way. Hearing the word come out of his mouth, he realizes she's right. "You know what, Ashley, you're right. I'm broken and flawed. And I hide behind my title and privilege to keep people from seeing it. I have bullied people and demeaned them so that I look and feel better about myself. I'm not the man people think I am. I'm sorry I let you down." He takes a step forward, "But I care about the people of this city. I care for the people I work with. Brohn here, and Ella. Elliot, Aarik and Sycilia."

"And Gwen," Ella adds.

"Right, and Gwen," Moses continues.

"Don't forget Hadvar," Brohn says.

"Yeah, obviously."

Ella intejects, "Also there's Posticker–"

"Everyone. I care about everyone here. And I do my best to take care of them, and the people around us. Look, I know you've got pain in your life, a past that haunts you, and you use it to justify hurting people, but you have to believe me, there is a better way to help the world than taking your anger out on it. Making yourself feel better by hurting others will only lead to more pain, more guilt, and more self-loathing."

The tip of Ashley's blade starts to shake.

"Please," Moses continues, "we can work together to help this girl. There's no need to kill her."

"Brohn?" an innocent voice says from Ella's hands.

Olive begins to wake and sees Ashely holding her sword toward Brohn. Olive's face twists into anger, and her eyes burn in black smoke. It pours out of her eyes and mouth, and she holds up her hands. A dark fog like dart propels from her palms and hits Ashley, knocking her down.

Olive's body then goes limp, instead of falling though, she begins to float out of Ella's grasp as the black fog spews forth. Brohn runs toward her.

"Olive," Brohn says. She lifts up past his head, and gloom spills on the ceiling.

"This is what I get for trusting you!" Ashley says standing back up, her armor half disintegrated, and her shoulder bloody. "To let my vow falter, I deserve this punishment, and I shall never again make this mistake!" She lifts her good arm A hand crossbow, cocked and ready to shoot, releases its bolt. The missile flies directly at the heart of the girl. The four men standing outside the tavern begin to push their way in, but Moses intercepts them.

Brohn jumps in the air and catches the bolt, spinning to absorb the momentum. He executes a three point landing between Ashley and Olive. Ashley grimaces, snarls, and grabs for her sword again. At the entrance, Moses stabs the first with his great sword, kicks the second one back into his allies, then closes the door.

"You two need to get her out of here. Follow the plan. I'll take care of the hunters," Moses commands.

"We can help you!" Ella argues as Ashley runs forward with an attack.

"I know you can," Moses says, locking the door and moving toward Ashley. "But she's more important than me, and you're the only one I trust to make sure she gets where she needs to go."

Ashley launches herself forward, and Moses blocks her. Ella pulls Olive toward the back door. The three witch hunters break the door of the tavern and stand ready to attack.

"Or," Moses says as he fights Ashely off, "you can make your own decision, 'cause you're an adult, and I want to empower you to do what you think is best. I respect you and all that you bring to the team.

"You don't want to fight all those dudes alone do you?" Ella says coming into the fight.

"I do not," Moses says as he trips Ashley onto the ground.

"No!" Ashley screams from the floor. "Destroy her or she will kill us all!" Ella looks at Ashley as she passes by. Pain, agony, longing, obsession.

Brohn shouts up to Olive, "Olive, if you can control this at all, focus on that guy right there." Brohn points at one of the two witch hunters charging them. Brohn takes the other one and tackles him to the ground. The last one leaps in the air to swing at the girl. A black tentacle slaps him and stuns him in the air. As he falls, the tentacle grabs his leg and throws him onto a table, smashing it and several of the man's bones.

"What have you done?!" Ashley screams as she stands up, her crimson cape hanging from one arm, her blade shining in the candle light of the tavern.

"Ashley, please stop. I don't want to have to hurt you," Moses pleads. Ashley runs forward and slashes at him. He deflects with his gauntlet. Ashley spins quickly and brings a dagger into Moses' leg. He screams out in pain, and Ashley begins to run toward the girl.

Brohn fights with the man who can't seem to land a dagger on Brohn's large chest. Ella crosses blades with the other Aberrant Hunter out classing his technique, but having a hard time with his strength.

From one knee, Moses' eyes shine in silver and a sudden rush of atmosphere blasts through the room. He holds out his hand, and suddenly Ashely stops moving.

"I have my own tricks, Ashley," Moses says. "I learned them from pushing myself through the paladin trials, from proving myself, from continuing to be a light to the people of this city. I don't justify murders with them; I use them to help." Her body turns in the air, and Moses can see that Ashley is crying.

"You have no idea what she will do, what they will all do. I just wanted to help. I just wanted to be like you, Moses."

"When you get back, they will be gone. You will never find her again, I can guarantee that," Moses says as he pulls a hair off his head. "I will be reporting this to the magecore. They can deem me unworthy if they like. It's a battle I've already fought. But you will not be welcome in this city anymore, I can tell you that."

"When I get back?" She asks. Moses ties the hair to his pointer and middle finger, Ashley's eyes widen in fear. "No, please, don't. A minute there is like a week."

"Good, it will be plenty of time to cool off," Moses says, pulling the string tight between his fingers. Ella loses her sword as her opponent crashes down on her. She waits for the moment as he lunges forward, then when it's right, dodges a forward strike and grabs his hand, using his moment against him.

"Moses, please," Ashley says.

Moses looks at her teary eyes, her flush face, the tremor in her hands. Her right hand moves slightly, beginning to break the spell that Moses has on her, when in a flash her wrist twists and a knife flies through the air. Moses dodges instinctually, moving

Witcher? I hardly know her.

his hand to deflect.

In the split second that the weapon passes, his hand moves in the way, and the knife cuts into the hair on his fingers. It slices through the air and with a popping noise, Ashley disappears.

The blade carries on and Ella moves the man around her body and catches the knife with his chest.

Brohn and his opponent go back and forth on attack, perry, swipe, move. Brohn jumps on the bar and handstands over the man's blade slash. Then grabs a bottle of booze and smashes it on the man's head. The man shakes it off and smiles. He readies his blade and lunges forward, stopping in mid air, as Olive grabs him with her black tendril. She then flicks him backward and out the tavern window.

Brohn looks up at the girl and smiles with a thumbs up. She looks back at him with a dark shadow covering her face and white eyes. A bright smile splits open and her hand moves to a thumbs up. She then falls unconscious again and begins to fall to the ground. Brohn moves quickly and grabs her. "Thanks Olive," he says as she sleeps in his arms. .

The city of Valeward:

The night is warm, children play around a fountain on the grass in a small park. A statue of a wise looking woman in flowing robes watches over the kids as they tag each other and run around.

On a bench is Moses. He wears a simple tunic and leather pants. The clothes of a normal citizen, the image that helps him blend in. He watches as the children play and he breathes in, relaxed and content.

"The future, right?" a voice says from behind him.

Moses turns around and sees Hadvar entering the park.

"Hey, barkeep, where have you been?" Moses asks. Hadvar sits down next to Moses, holding a book in his lap.

"When Gwen was born, I was knocked on my ass. I couldn't believe it. I gave up everything for her. To the point where I gave her up." Hadvar turns to Moses, "She lived on the Hallowed Coast with her aunt and uncle until I figured out my life here."

"I didn't realize that."

"I gave up everything for her," Hadvar turns back to the kids. "But what I didn't realize was that giving up a part of me could cost her and everyone so much. There was so much I should have done, and I'm destined to do."

"You're not gonna like, blow yourself up right?" Moses asks, getting uncomfortable with the conversation.

"Haha, no," Hadvar says."I just know what it's like to sacrifice to make things right. But I think it's time Moses. You start to understand that you don't need to sacrifice who you are to do good. For your family and friends, or for the city." Hadvar rubs the book in his lap, leather bound and thick.

"I think it's time you meet a good friend of mine. Someone that knows what it means to sacrifice what he loves for others."

"You're not going to recruit me to the Salvationists are you?"

"No." Hadvar stands up, turns around and lifts his hand in an introductory way, "This is my friend."

Moses turns around to see a figure in a dark cloak, black hair that glimmers with stars, a pale gaunt face and a stoic expression. Moses stands up.

"My name is Grimander," the figure says in a smooth

and expressionless tone, "It's good to finally meet you."

"What's going on?" Moses says, "Hadvar, what are you doing with an Arch Fey?"

"You know what he is?"

"I'm a paladin," Moses says. "I study." He pauses, then looks at Grimander. "Well, Elliot studies. And he talks to me about the stuff he finds most interesting. Androgynous dudes with sparkling hair rings a few bells."

"I've known him for a long time," Hadvar says, "and I think it would be beneficial for you to hear his offer."

"Offer?" Moses asks. "From a fey lord?"

"For the sake of your..." Grimander pauses and looks past Moses, "future." Moses looks back at the children. A young boy no older than four plays with the other children, laughing and running. A slight gleam of silver in his eyes.

Moses chews on his lip, then turns back to the dark creature before him. "Might as well talk over a drink."

"Great!" Hadvar says. "Let's head to the Penny Lich." They begin walking with Hadvar putting a hand on Moses' shoulder. "How's Brohn doing? Taking care of the place? I told him that it better be perfectly clean when I get back."

Moses hisses, "About that, I have a story to tell you."

T.W. CLAWSON

THE
PENNY LICH

A FANTASY SITCOM

The Way of
Dragon Kings

Day one in the Temple:

Elliot the Cleric, Sycilia Willowmight, her twin brother Aarik Willowmight, and Gwen Yong are led through the decrepit tomb of the Dragon King by Primo Andarsen. He says, "As you can see by the columns we've built as supports for the entrance, e've been at this project for some time. We enlisted the work of the Ironhide Dwarves after we completed our entryway columns."

"They sure are..." Sycilia stumbles. "Uh, very nice pillars."

"Yes, well, they are recreations of what we believe to be the original relief," Primo Andarsen says. Elliot is taking in every ounce of the room, and even pulls out parchment and charcoal. As Andarsen continues, Elliot gets farther and farther away from the group, taking notes, rubbing the designs into his notebook.

"So do you guys ever, like...party in here?" Aarik asks.

"What?" Andarsen grimaces.

"Like, bring some baddies down here to hang and chill?"

"Why would they do that?" Sycilia says.

"It just seems like a super cool place for a low key hang, Moses would know what I'm talking about," Aark says, touching a design.

"Please don't touch that." Andarsen reaches forward. "It took us years to carve these, using the most exact measurements and pouring over ancient scrolls to guide us in what the Sandren Temple looked like."

"Yeah, it's not a party place," Sycilia says.

"Bummer." Aarik kicks a rock.

"Through that door, we'll enter the open grounds, where the Ironhide clan has done wonders to create a comfortable space for us to live. In fact the lake is a natural...." He trails off, Sycilia being the only one to listen. Elliot continues to sketch, Poststicker sitting on his shoulder.

"What do you think, buddy? Does that look like the same dragon crawling up the side of this thing? " He looks up at Potsticker, who looks between him and the drawing. Closes his eyes and shakes his head.

"I knew it. I need to get closer and do a trace," Elliot says, crumpling up the paper.

"Now before we go through the great hall door, I just want to remind you that while the temple grounds are open to all of you, we have to take precautions to keep things from deteriorating further," Primo Andarsen says.

"Why are you looking at me?" Aarik says.

"Because I told you not to touch anything and you're currently leaning on the Mother Dragon's rump."

Aarik looks at his support and realizes that the stone is a dragon statue that leaves nothing to imagination on anatomical correctness.

"Right," Aarik says, wiping his hand off, "Ok."

"I just need to get this last part," Elliot says, standing on his tippy toes to get the etching of the design above his head. He doesn't notice that the rock below the pillar he is leaning on is loose, shuffling outward under his pressure.

"So, like I said," Primo Andarsen says in the small shaft of light streaming in from the outside, the great hall door behind him carved from wood and gems, "We are happy to have you all here, but be sure to treat this place like the jewel it is... When in doubt, do as Elliot would do." The man looks about. "Uh, where is Elliot?"

"I honestly thought you were Elliot for a second there," Aarik says.

"Yeah, where is he?" Sycilia adds.

"I got it," Elliot hisses at Potsticker. "I got the etch, forever saved in my notebook. This is gonna be—" The rocks he's standing on gives out and pushes on the rocks holding the pillar up. A loud crack resounds through the cavernous room.

"Nononono," Elliot says as he grabs onto the pillar in front of him. As it begins falling, it pulls Elliot forward, crashing into the ground and hitting the next pillar over. That column, covered replications in centuries of lost art and culture, smashes into rubble, scattering to the next column over. This pillar breaks and falls as a solid massive wrecking ball and continues the line of demolition.

Primo Andarsen watches as the entire rounded front entryway of the Sandren Temple slowly gives way to gravity and breaks down to rubble. The grinding, cracking, booming, and subsequent repeat of said sounds accompanies the realization that years of labor and research are gone, within moments.

Finally the last column rests near the party. Dust begins to settle and they look at the destruction brought down. Standing at the base of the first column is El-

liot, and standing on the toppled structure is Potsticker. The group looks at Elliot for a moment, he adjusts
his glasses, and without turning to look, he points his
figure at Potsticker.

Potsticker shutters in surprise, then hops. He then
takes one of his fury nubs and points it back at Elliot.
Elliot sees this and chuckles nervously.

"His pants are on fire, so you know he's a liar." He
claps his hands together, "Anywho, who is ready for
some dwarven lunch? I hear they make the best hot
meat sandwiches." Potsticker bounces up and down
several times and then jumps out of sight.

Week one in the Temple:
"I'm about to lose my mind, bro," Sycilia says. She
sits with her back to the massive cavern within the
Sandren Temple. The hollowed out mountain was
home to one of the greatest kings in recorded history
of Yonder Valley. The Dragon Sandren. He who fought
the Abberents from the southern desert. He who made
alliance with the elves of the west, and made for them
a crystal kingdom to the north.

His likeness is carved into a great statue that stands
several stories tall, looking over a small underground
lake. A river breaks at his head and streams on either
side of it, falling to a lake below to where the base
camp of the Mission of Knowledge has been built on
the banks.

It is made of several blocks of tents and temporary
structures. Like the nomadic tribes on the Valward
Tundra, they built around individual fires and walk-
ways were made from the area between the small
collections of shelters cluttered together.

Most stayed at least a few hundred feet from the water, but still the encampment sprawls out around the entirety of the lake's radius.

The greatness of the Draco King stands as a reminder to the monks who walk about the vacant halls and ancient rooms; that they are here for a reason. Greatness and legacy are always staring at them, and it is their duty to pry truth and history from the very rocks this mountain is built from.

"This place sucks," Sycilila says as she takes a swig of her drink. Then she reconsiders. "The ale is good though."

"Sycilia, come on, dude," Aarik says. "Look at this place. It's full of mystery and story and history and...."

"And magic," Sycilia finishes for him.

"Yeah, somewhere in there," Aarik says.

"You've had a hard on for magic items since we got here, and you haven't found anything."

"I just haven't been on the right runs yet."

"You go on every run!" Sycilia says. "Meanwhile, I'm here, watching Elliot pour over every book ever written on one guy."

"Come on, it's not that bad."

"Have you seen this place?!" Sycilia shouts. "All the rooms have a thousand books and they all talk about him!" She points to the statue. "And Elliot has to read every single one of them. He's insane."

"He's excited," Aarik retorts.

"He's obsessed." Sycilia takes a swig, and wipes her face with her forearm. "It's so annoying, all day and all night. Hmm, oh, interesting, wow, hmm." She mocks him. "What a fascinating view. Oh wow, this changes everything. Hmm, oh wow."

"Yeah, he's a huge nerd, you knew that when you signed up for this job."

"I thought it was going to be adventure and dungeon

delving, not watching a pansy little twerp read his fanfiction."

"Uhhh...Should I leave?" Elliot says from the opposite side of the table, no more than four feet from the conversation.

A moment passes as Aarik looks at Elliot. Elliot pushes his glasses up, his blond hair in a messy bun, his eyes concerned about what he hears.

"What?" Aarik asks. "No, you're fine man. Keep doing your thing."

"Ok, but it seems like you really don't like me doing my thing," Elliot says, pointing to his book.

"I'm fine with it," Aarik says. "It's really only Sycilia that has a problem with it. Anyway/" Aarik turns back to Sycilia. "At some point I'll make sure I stay back and babysit the squishy, so you can explore. This place is crazy cool."

"I don't know," Sycilia replies. "I'm not sure you can handle him." Elliot tries to focus on reading."He's super needy. 'Sycilia, I'm gonna get some food,' 'Sycilia I need to use the bathroom,' 'Sycilia I'm ready for bed.'"

"Seriously, I can just go." Elliot starts to get up.

"Do your work, dude," Sycilia says.

"It's just, it seems weird that you're having this conversation right in front of me."

"Would you rather we talk about you behind your back?" Aarik asks.

"Well...." Elliot thinks about it, then submits to the logic, "I mean, yeah, I guess." He looks between the both of them.

They look at each other, and shrug. Sycilia gets up and Aarik starts walking. "Alright, bro," Aarik says as they make their way from in front of Elliot. The Cleric goes back to his book, and sighs as he starts reading again. He's unaware, as he reads, that Aarik and Sycilia walk around to the table directly behind him. Closer now than when they had been in front of him.

"You see what I'm saying?" Sycilia says. "He's like always on. He's constantly talking to me about stuff that I just couldn't care less about." Elliot realizes they're there and looks up in confusion.

"I mean, it sounds like you need to let him know, somehow," Aarik says. "Like strike up a conversation with him and let him know that he's probably the most boring man on the planet, and you'd rather run into the dark than listen to him prattle on about the most meaningless things."

"I can," Elliot starts, "uh, I can still hear you."

"What's up?" Sycilia says, turning around.

"I get it, I get it," Elliot says.

"What's that, bro?" Aarik asks.

"The next time the Ironhides find a new cavern, I would like Sycilia to go on the delve," Elliot says. "I get it. Aarik you can stay here."

"Yes!" Sycilia says in victory.

"What? Come on!" Aarik shouts in anger.

"There you go," Elliot says. "Now please, let me go back to my studies."

"Yeah, of course," Sycilia says happily.

Elliot turns back around and begins reading. He makes it a few lines in when he hears from behind him.

"Can you believe he did that?" Aarik asks. "I mean, who does he think he is?"

"I don't know, bro," Sycilia says. "You should probably talk to him about it." Elliot sighs in frustration.

Gwen is cooking. That's all she does, that's all she is good for. Cooking, cleaning, and watching Potsticker.

She breathes out as she works on a stew from the party's camp. A carriage with a couple tents around a fire pit, all next to the underground lake. The cool air from the lake fights the heat of the fire, and the view is spectacular. Balcony above balcony, above more balconies, looking down at the great wide courtyard. There are rooms and tunnels dug into the stone from this main chamber, and monks from all over the world come to explore. Torches, lanterns, lamps, and arcane beacons hang from the balconies and massive columns. The arcane beacons filled the empty air, finding wanderers and providing light to them as they walked.

"Here I am, in one of the most mysterious places in the world, and I'm cooking traverler's stew," she grumbles, looking down at Potsticker. In the fire pit, he sits below the cauldron and forces heat to cook the broth. He puts his lip out and Gwen reacts with the same expression.

"Don't get me wrong, hon, I love being with you, but I thought I might come here and get some answers, you know?"

Poststicker crawls forward, leaving a fire behind on the wood. Gwen puts her hand up and lets him crawl up. His nubbed little feet stand on her hands, and she brings him close.

"I know, I know, I shouldn't complain. But I want to figure some things out. That's why I came. Just look at that epic figure." They turn and look up at the statue. The statue is grand and imposing. Gwen wonders if the term 'king' is right for the person carved.

"I'm just saying it's fine," a voice says from around the carriage. Gwen quickly puts Posticker down and waits for Elliot to round the corner. Aarik is with him and they come to a stop when they see her.

"Hey Aarik," Gwen says, rubbing her toe in the dirt.

"Hey Gwen." Aarik smiles at her.

"Hey Gwen. Oh uh, Potstsicker, don't get too close to

her," Elliot says a bit too sternly. The flame creature runs back to the fire pit and hides under the cauldron.

"He's ok," Gwen says.

"I just don't want him to hurt you." Elliot walks over to the pit, "I can handle the heat, since I'm his guardian, but if any of you touch him, your skin will melt off the bone in an instant." Elliot bends down and puts his hands out. Potsticker comes out and rubs on Elliot's hand, closing his feline face.

"I have to protect him at all costs, but I also have to protect the world from him. It's terrifying."

"So true." Aarik says, "I knew a guy in Haberdashery Woods who was a single father and it was a full time gig, so, you know, kudos to you."

'There's harder jobs out there," Elliot replies. "Plus, I'm not his dad. I'm a guardian entrusted with this safety and upbringing by a Deity of the Hollowed Conclave. So you know, a little stressful."

"I dunno, he seems pretty sweet," Gwen says as Potsticker rubs on Elliots legs.

"Sure, he seems like it, but he's a lot to handle, and I already have enough on my plate."

"With wh–?" Gwen asks, but Aarik jumps in.

"No, don't ask!" Aarik looks frustrated, "Now he's gonna talk about it."

"About what?"

"The door," Aarik says.

"The door?" Gwen asks.

"THE DOOR!" Elliot seethes with anger. He points to a massive door at the feet of the Sandren statue. As tall as two men and as wide as four, a set of stairs ascend from the lake to a small platform in front of the door. Jewels are encrusted in the ornate weaving pattern of it. Made of metal, it gleams, untarnished, uninjured.

"When the two come together, as fire and water, the blood of the elemental planes and the blood of the woods will seal this door; only their bond can make way," Elliot recites in a regal and poised speech. Aark rolls his eyes. "Shut behind is the dark, the lord of something something I never made out, and then it ends with... and my children shall inherit the burden; forever be vigil for the Sandren's line shall forever be magical."

"Its a dumb door that no one can open," Aarik sums up.

"I will figure it out, Aarik," Elliot says.

"And in the meantime I'll watch you read book after book," Aarik sulks. "Since you're letting Sycilia go on the next delve."

"You know there's a lot of books around here that have clues as to where you can find magic items."

"Wait, what?!" Aarik throws his arms out. "This whole time you've been hobgoblining the good books?"

"Hobgoblining?" Gwen asks.

"No, I mean they're everywhere, you can just pick one up," Elliot says as Aarik starts looking through the books.

"Well, it's time," Sycilia says, walking up to the group with her sword in hand and several more pieces of armor on her arms and legs.

"Time for what?" Gwen asks.

"Time to go exploring," Sycilia says. "The Ironhides found a new sealed off location. Any advice Aarik?"

"Don't find any magic items, they're for me," he says looking at a book.

"Not if I get to it first." Sycilia kisses Aarik on the top of the head. "One for you." She turns to Gwen and kisses her on the head. "One for you." She then turns to Elliot and begins to lean down for a kiss, but Elliot stands up quickly.

"Er, eh...Good luck," Elliot says, putting his hand out. Sycilia looks at the hand, and Aarik smirks at them.

"Thanks," Sycilia takes the hand and shakes it.

"Please be safe. I could never replace you," Elliot says as he holds her hand. Clammy, still shaking up and down.... The shake slows, but Elliot continues to hold.

"Uh, oh. Ok," Sycilia says, letting the handhold continue.

"Right, well." Elliot does not break the moment.

"I should probably get going," Sycilia says. They still hold hands. Elliot looks down and sees this, his face changes to terror.

He pulls his hand back quickly. "Right, I have to be good too, also good, good too. Goodbye." He begins walking away quickly, taking his book and Potsticker with him.

"Have fun reading your books?" Sycilia asks, awkwardly.

"Yup, you too!" Elliot shouts without looking back.

"You too?" Aarik asks.

"I dunno." Sycilia looks at her brother. "Hey, you better take care of him. Don't be an ass to him either."

Aarik points a finger at her. "And I'm serious. Don't take my magic items."

Sycilia begins walking off, raising her eyebrows back and forth.

"I know that look Sycilia," Aarik shouts after her from their table. "Those are my magic items. Don't you take them."

She winks.

"This is not gonna be like Griffy! You're not gonna

get away with this!" he yells. She disappears around a corner, waving him off. He settles down and then turns to see Gwen.

"What?"

"Griffy?" She asks.

"My stuffed Griffin. She stole it from me after I won it at a carnival."

"Still holding onto that?" She asks.

"I mean, yeah. He sleeps next to my bed, to protect me from nightmares."

"Haha, I meant the loss of your doll, not the doll itself." She gets up, laughing as she leaves.

Aarik calls out, "it's not a doll!" She leaves and he speaks to himself quietly, "It's a collectible."

Sycilia holds the torch up to the cavern wall, seeing the rough marks made by the dwarves as they broke the rocks that filled this hallway only a day ago.

"I have to be honest," one of the dwarves says, "I was expecting Aarik to come with us."

"I'm sorry to disappoint you," Sycilia says.

"Not a disappointment," The dwarf continues as they head through the dark. "Honestly, while I think your brother is great, it's nice to be working with another woman."

"There's another woman on this delve?" Sycilia asks.

"Of course!" the dwarf stops, the flame catches up to the torch and fires upward. "Me!" The dwarf turns around and Sycilia realizes the companion before her is indeed a womanly dwarf. Her body is rough and bulky like the men of her race, and her hair short, shorter than the men in fact. Her eyes shimmer in a feminine fashion, in a way that Sycilia had a hard time understanding. More understanding. More connected than the men of her kind.

"The hair threw me off," Sycilia said suddenly, trying to find awkward excuses. "Also, I guess I never met a dwarf woman."

"Have you ever seen a dwarven military before?"

"No. In Valley Gate and Valeward I've only really seen the... eh, what are they called? The guards that watch over the palaces and embassies?"

"The Golem Guard?"

"Yeah, that's it."

"That's us!" The woman says, she begins walking.

"Us?" Sycilia follows.

"The Golem Guard are all women." Her voice echoes around her body as she leads them through the cave.

"In the big metal suits?"

"Aye. Our Tradition dictates that a woman can show no skin or eye when not in the mountain."

"So you have to wear full plate mail when you're not underground?"

"Aye."

"Doesn't that get...uncomfortable?"

"Yeah, which is why most of us stay below." The woman gestures to the rocks. "In here, I'm free to run about as I see fit."

Sycilia shakes her head, "That's awful. You're suppressed by the men of your culture, forced to live life according to their made up rules."

The dwarven woman laughs. "I like you." She then spins about and faces Sycilia, standing at her chest. "Reckeshali Don Esheedehnali." She holds out her hand, "You can call me Recky."

Sycilia takes the hand. "Sycilia Willowmight."

Recky smiles and breaks the hand shake. "I know you skywatchers think we've been oppressed, but our people are governed by the matriarchy."

"You have women running the culture, and you still

exact harsh laws against yourselves."

Recky turns and leads Sycilia through the darkness, "Our men never wear the sacred armor. Armor that belonged to them many years ago, by the way. They are forbidden. Who is the law against then? They can never attain the status of a Golem Guard, nor can they lead as a Chief or Governor, or obviously Matriarch."

"But you can never go outside in regular clothes."

"We are born of the rock, we sleep in the dark, we breathe the dust. We are not the same as you sky-watchers. We love the feel of our home, the Under-realm. Sure, some men venture out into the world above to find fortunes, but the rock below has as many treasures as the trees."

"It all seems designed to keep the world from seeing you."

"Exactly!" Recky shouts, her ample voice bounces. "Only the men who dig and fight the earth for its trea-sures, the men who live below and within our rule are allowed to see us. The sun, the men above, the ones that have yet to earn their place in the heart of the world, they will never see the beauty and voluptuous figures we dwarven women offer the world. We are a prize." Recky continues to lead, as Sycilia thinks and follows.

"You still back there?" Recky asks.

"I am. I'm just very conflicted" Sycilia says.

"Why's that?"

"I spent so long trying to gain my independence, and I still am. And I just can't see how forcing yourselves to cover up in public can be freeing. It goes against everything I stand for. My father telling me what I can and can't do, the men who pursued me and tried to make me something they thought was better for me, and now having to work for the government so that

I can earn my place in this world. And then you tell me that there are women who want to be held to this standard. They choose the life of...being...I dunno, you say it's not oppression, but I can't think of anything else."

"I understand, Sycilia. I do," Recky says, turning to look Sycilia in the eye. "But there is freedom in a bond. Something that forces you to be more than yourself. A freedom in knowing that you can be more. My sisters and I have that bond. One day you will find that too, perhaps with your guild, or a man, or woman. It's about denying yourself, and finding how much better you are on the other side of it." Recky winks and continues walking.

"I'm happy to know that dwarven women are so beautiful," Sycilia says. "And really, just exist at all, to be honest."

"Haha! What'd you think? The men all mated with each other?"

"That or they just found new ones while they dug in the rock!" Sycilia laughs. They both chuckle for a minute, and enjoy the moment.

"Well, now comes the fun part." Recky moves the torch around and reveals a drop off. The cavern opens up to a massive hole leading down into nothingness. Sycilia gets closer to the edge, holding her torch over it.

"What's down there?" Sycilia asks.

"The Underrealm," Recky says.

"Really? How do we get down there?"

"Like this." Recky then pushes Sycilia off the ledge, watching her fall into the darkness, her scream fading long after she disappears.

Sycilia falls through the darkness. Every so often she

can see a small bit of light off in the distance, in the direction she thinks she's falling toward. As the gleam grows, it becomes a bioluminescent mushroom growing on the side of the pit. An odd bit of vertigo sets in every time she passes one.

"Isn't this fun!?" a voice says from behind her. Recky holds a twinkling gem that sheds bright green light all around her.

Sycilia turns in the air, her black and white dreads flailing around her. She opens her mouth to speak, but all that comes out is a howl of terror.

"Neverbeen to the Underrealm, I presume," Recky shouts over the winds rushing past them.

Sycilia screams again.

"You'll be fine. In a minute here you'll feel a sudden change. Like you hit water and your body is ready to move back the other way. You'll feel sick. It happens to everyone the first time."

"Why are we going down here?" Sycilia manages to ask.

"The men found this hole. We confirmed it's a commuter tunnel and need to see what's at the other end of it. Seems the Draco King had a connection to the Underrealm that no one knew about."

"This is not what I signed up for!"

"You're right," Recky says, laughing. "It's better!"

After a moment, Sycilia feels the change that Recky described.

"There it is," Recky says, "We just passed the apex. We are now fighting gravity. We will be ascending for about as long as we were descending, and then you'll want to hold me at the pinnacle of our commute."

Sycilia feels the sudden lurching of her stomach fill her mouth with agony and bile. "I'm gonna throw up."

"Throw down!"

Sycilia twists her body and hurls her food below them. In the oddest sight she's ever seen, the spew travels along with her slightly, then globulates into bubbles and then speeds back into the darkness they came from.

Recky brings up her arm. A gauntlet with a small crank and crossbow reflects light. She takes a metal string from her belt and attaches it to the bolt on the crossbow, then aims it.

"You're gonna want to hold onto me."

"Where?" Sycilia begins to panic.

"You see these hips, girl? They're for grabbin;! Let's go!" Sycilia wills herself over to Recky and grabs ahold of the belt around her waist. At that moment the world catches up to them and pulls back. Sycilia's hair flies back up and she feels her stomach lurch again. Recky fires the bolt, an echoing zing of the crank letting the wire spool outward, and then the sound of sharp entry into a rock.

The ladies fall a moment, and then hang from the wire attached to the belt. Sycilia holds on for her life, realizing that she had snuggled into the dwarven woman's body. She looks up and sees Recky smiling.

"Pretty fun, right?" she asks.

"No, not particularly," Sycilia answers honestly.

"We can do it again. All I have to do is cut this bo—"

"No!" Sycilia shouts. "I mean...." She calms down. "Please for the love of all that's holy, no."

"Alright," Recky says. She then takes a second wire from her belt and attaches it to a new bolt, aims in front of her and shoots. The bolt takes anchor, and when Recky starts cranking the spool, they begin to edge toward the hole in the wall, entering the Under-realm.

Gwen comes back to the camp to see Elliot and Potsticker playing. Elliot takes a piece of food and throws it in the air, as Potctticker jumps, flips, and eats the food. Elliot cheers him on, then points to a small dummy. There are several set up around the area, some of them having burn marks, others looking brand new, and some looking burned to hell.

"Whatca doin'?" Gwen asks, as she sits at a table near Elliot. She realizes that there's a dummy on the table only after it's too late. A flame roars past her, engulfing the straw and mud thing, burning it to ashes.

"We're training," Elliot says, throwing a piece of food at his ward. The living flame creature jumps in the air, bites it and after landing gives a little howl. "That's right, buddy," Elliot says, "We're gonna make sure no one messes with you. And also, you know, help you not burn down our entire camp."

"Hmmm, Interesting." Gwen says. Elliot turns to see that she has a glazed over look, her head on her hand, leaning on the table. He looks in the direction of her gaze and sees Aarik reading a book and throwing daggers at a wooden post. Elliot's eyebrows raise. Smiling, he walks over to her. Potsticker whines slightly, and Elliot absentmindedly throws a bit of food down, Potsticker trailing behind him.

"So, I was thinking we would switch up dinner tonight," Elliot says.

"Mhhhm."

"Like, maybe we would cook one of the dwarves," Elliot tries.

"Yeah? Sounds good to me."

"Maybe slather a dead dwarf with some cranberry sauce and serve him to the local camps?"

"Whatever you think," Gwen says absentmindedly.

"And then maybe we write a book, Fifty New Ways to Cook a Dwarf, and serve him to his friends."

"You're on fire today."

"Good Divine, you're distracted," Elliot snaps and gets Gwen's attention. "Hello? Welcome to the conversation."

"What?" Gwen takes her eyes off Aarik and sees Elliot.

"Do you even realize what you agreed to?" Elliot asks.

"Cooking a Dwarf, feeding him to his friends, and co-authoring a book with you." She smiles. "I'm distracted, not deaf."

"What's going on? You like him?" Elliot nods to Aarik.

"I mean...."

"I knew it!" Elliot points excitedly. "I knew it, for once I knew something about someone, and Moses didn't. Ha!"

"First of all, you need to chill. A crush only works if the other person isn't immediately informed of it," Gwen says, pulling Elliot back down. Potsticker pulls at Elliot's leg, Elliot throws a little more food down. "Secondly, it's not that big a deal."

"I mean, maybe not for you. But I never know about these things," Elliot says.

"Yeah, I could tell."

"Why don't you go talk to him?"

"What would I talk about?" Gwen asks. "Oh, hey Aarik, isn't that a lovely rock? Oh, look Aarik, a bug is crawling over the table. What are your thoughts on the Hallowed Conclave? Do you follow the tenets of all the Divine, or just the ones that pertain to you? Face it, there's nothing interesting for us to talk about down here." She sighs. Yet around her, waterfalls crash over a statue of the great dragon king, magical lights float like fireflies through the vast cavern, and around a small underground lake is a temporary city filled with Monks and Clerics of Knowledge. "...this place is boring."

Potsticker raps at Elliots leg, and Elliot pushes the creature down and puts the food on the table next to the burned dummy.

"You can talk to him about anything. If he likes you back, he's gonna just enjoy you talking to him."

"Are you seriously trying to give me advice right now, Elliot?"

"I mean, I've been married, so I know about...getting...the girls."

"Did you ever 'get' Ella?"

Lines crossover Elliot's face, and he contemplates how to answer, but Gwen can see it all, and he gives up. "No, We never did it. Our marriage was a sham, and she was only really using me to help her kill a monster."

"I deal with guys everyday at work. I know what men are like, trust me."

"I'm just saying, he's available, you're available, you two would be good together."

"Elliot, there's more to it than that."

"Like what?"

"Its just, there's stuff about me that...." She sighs. "I don't know if I can deal with that right now."

"What's going on?" Elliot's face changes. His eyes engage in a way that Gwen has rarely seen. A serenity. He cocks his head a little and purses his lips in a way that makes him look funny in a cute sort of way. He really wants to help.

"There's this thing that I've had to figure out about myself, I'm–" As Gwen begins talking, Potsticker jumps on the table. He begins to grab at the food, and his heat burns what remains of the dummy.

"What the Hells!?" Elliot grabs at the flame creature, but it jumps back. Tripping on itself, Potsticker rolls backward and directly into Gwen. She catches Potsticker, and Elliot sees contact between the girl and the elemental. Gwen quickly throws Potsticker on the ground and stands up.

"Oh my Diety, Oh Divines!" Elliot says rushing over to Gwen. "Sweet Harelds, I'm so sorry!" Tears begin forming in his eyes as he comes around the table to Gwen. He then sees that apart from a little clothing getting scorched, she is fine. No burns, no melted skin, no blackened charcoaled body parts. She looks up at Elliot and smiles.

"Gwen what, what, whatwhatwhat?" Elliot can't get his words to work.

"You know what?" Gwen says, "I think I will talk to Aarik. Bye!" Gwen quickly leaves and starts walking past the table toward Aarik.

"Gwen, wait, what? Wait!"

"Oh, looks like he caught the table on fire," Gwen says, not turning around to look at Elliot. She discreetly points her finger at the table, as she walks by and a small bolt of fire launches from her to the wood. Immediately it catches fire and burns brightly.

"Oh, come on," Elliot shouts.

'You got this? Ok I'm gonna go talk to Aarik, love you byyyyeee!" Gwen says as she shuffles away.

In the Underrealm:
Recky takes an orb out of her backpack and speaks a command word. It lights up, breaks into a hundred smaller bits, and fills the air around them.

"Neon scatter orb," Recky says. She smiles at the

delight on Sycilia's face. Sycilia then turns to the left and her face drops in horror.

"What's that?" She asks. Recky turns to look at what Sycilia points to. She shakes the last piece of the orb in her hand, and the lights in the air shift. Decorations made of black stone reflect the lights. Pillars like the entrance way, carved with dragons and great serpents. A grand statue of a dragon lounges about the room, its neck leading to a great open mouth close the ground. The hilt of a sword protrudes out of the mouth of the carving.

Several doors carve their way farther into the mountain. And then the sight of the floor brings terror and the smell of death. Sycilia gasps as she looks down and sees the multitude of bodies laying on the ground. Recky quickly runs to the closest one.

"Dead," Recky says, as Syscilia tries to count the bodies. Too many. The smell begins to get to her.

"How?" Sycilia asks.

"I can't say for sure, but look," Recky beckons Syscila over and points to the eyes. Sycilia gasps again.

"Their eyes are missing. And the black goo, what is that?" Sycilia asks.

"I would say," Recky puts the head of the man down, "that's his eyes."

"Melted?"

"Possibly?"

"Was this the dragon? Sandren?" Sycillia looks up at the intimidating statue. There's something on each tooth of the dragon. A band of some kind.

"No. I mean, I don't know for sure. But these men have been dead no longer than a day or two."

Sycilia looks down at a new body. She twists the corpse's nose and checks his ears. Opening his mouth, she checks his teeth and tongue. "At least they've been preserved to look that way. But I think you're right."

"Now we just have to figure out what killed them."

"Check this out." Sycilia holds up a hand. The man she inspects has a worn wooden ring on his finger. "Check the other bodies," Sycilia says. Recky does so.

"Every single one, They all have a ring. Was this a cult?"

"No." Sycilia pulls the ring off the corpse. "No, this was something else. I've seen this before."

"A room full of dead guys? With melted eyes? Who do you hang out with?" Recky asks as Sycilia examines the wooden ring. The same markings on the outside. And new ones on the inside. Sycilia begins walking toward the mouth of the dragon, taking in the blade in the mouth and the things on the teeth.

Each tooth has a ring fitted on it, etched with runes, glowing in magic. Sycilia's heart drops. Next to the dragon's mouth is a barrel, closed and marked with the name, 'Waller'.

"Yes, master." A voice echoes from one of the hallways leading away from the room. The two women look at each other. Sycilia points to Recky in question, Reacky shakes her head and points at Sycilia, Sycilia shakes her head. They both look toward the cave-like a hallway.

"I'm heading there now, master," the voice says as it begins to break the darkness. "The blade room. Yes. They are all dead. I will be sure to hurry." The figure, speaking a one-sided conversation, comes out into the light of the bioluminescent mushrooms, allowing Sycilia and Recky to see him from their improvised hiding space. They poke their heads out from behind the dragon's feet and immediately Sycilia's blood boils.

"You gotta be kidding me," She hisses.

"What? Do you know him?" Recky whispers back.

"Yes. His name is Noodle, and he's a massive A-hole."

Noodle the Wild Elf, balding and bearded, long sharp ears and short stature, walks among the dead in the temple room. He bends over and begins pulling the rings off the bodies.

"There's quite a few of them here, master," he says as he struggles to rip one off. "Seems you had a lot o' men working for you before I showed up. No, no, no, nothing. I mean nothing by it, master. I'm meanin' that if we can reenergize these rings as you say, then I could have a lot more help. No, don't say that, master, I'm happy doing the work, anything to earn my fair share. Wait a minute." Noodle stops as he looks at a body. He looks around, his elven eyes piercing into the dark. "This body is missing a ring," he says. "You haven't sent anyone else up here to collect have you? Of course, master." He closes his eyes and breathes steadily for a moment, then his ears twitch slightly.

"And then, he called me a racist. Can you believe that? So then we won the bar from him and he disappeared, but not before he left an entire gang that was selling onerings for us to deal with," Sycilia gossips from their hiding place.

"Well, well, well," Noodle says as he peers around the legs. The ladies stand up straight and come out, armed. "If it isn't...uh, that one girlie I fought that one time."

"Sycilia Willowmight," Sycilia says.

"Sure, whateva."

"You seriously don't remember me? I destroyed your life, sent you running for the hills, and tattered your name."

"Eh, shit happens, love. You were just a catalyst for the world to work."

"I can't believe it. You forgot me that fast?"

"Is this really that important?" Recky asks.

"Kinda, yeah. What happened between us, it changed my life."

"You're welcome darlin'," Noodle says, "But to be honest, I have that effect on many women."

"Eww!" Sycilia shouts. "Not like that, you pig."

"What happened to these men?" Recky tries to get back on track.

"What was promised to them," Noodle says. "They were given great power, and then they gave themselves to The Finger Beast."

"The Finger Beast?" Sycilia asks.

"The Great Old One from below Yonder Valley," Noodle says. "His Harold has begun the work, and soon the world will be touched by the dark tendrils of my glorious deity."

"Gross. Don't say a finger monster is going to touch people," Sycilia says. Recky agrees with a sour face.

"That's not," Noodle stammers, "No, that's not what I meant."

"It doesn't matter what you meant," Sycilia says. "We're stopping you here." Sycilia holds her blade up and prepares to attack. "Be careful, Recky. He has the Blade of Mable. It's incredibly dangerous."

"Wrong on two accounts, love." Noodle holds up his hand, no blade, no weapon. Instead on his finger is a ring. It's made of metal and glows in magic runes. "I lost the blade when I signed on with a new employer. Which is fine, 'cause I got this instead. The second thing? You're never gonna stop me, Waller, or The Finger Beast!"

"Waller?" Sycilia hesitates for a moment. In the split second, a black spectral hand reaches out from Noodle's ring and grabs ahold of her. Wrapping its darkened fingers around her body, it keeps her still. Another hand takes Sycilia's sword and tosses it to the other side of the room

Recky wastes no time shooting a bolt from her gauntlet and charging with an ax. The bolt deflects as a black disruption in the air rebounds and shimmers. Noodle laughs.

The darkness from his ring leaks out and begins to orbit around him. The dwarven warrior fights the streaming blackness that swirls about. She swings and slices through, but it reforms and hits her in the face.

Noodle then summons a dark blade from the ring, energy forming around his hand. He brings the blade up to cut at Recky's neck, but as he does, Sycilia strikes.

She had dropped from the hold and grabbed the nearest blade she could. It had slid from the dragon's mouth like it was nothing. She swung it into an arc and jumped for her attack.

Her blade deflects the dark sword and knocks Noodle backward. The black blade looks diminished from the hit. Noodle's eyes grow wild at the sight of the sword in Sycilia's hand. He tries to stabilize, but Recky is already on top of him. She grabs his body and begins holding him down.

"Give me that blade! It belongs to Waller!!" Noodle screams.

Sycilia takes the opportunity and grabs the elf's ringed hand.

"What are you doing?" Noodle shouts. "No!" He tries to summon another black bolt, but Recky punches him in the face.

"Do it now!" Recky shouts. Sycilia groans as she pries open Noodle's hand and tries to pull the ring off.

"It won't budge!"

"Master, they are trying to take you from me! elp your servant! Give me the power to take back your blade!"

"Cut it off," Recky demands. Sycilia looks up for a moment, feels the energy beginning to radiate from the magic item. She grimaces, and then moves her blade to the finger.

Slink!

"Noooooo!" Noodle screams, then curls up. Sycilia takes the ring and finger and moves away from the elf. Recky backs away, watching as the elf mumbles and cries. He holds his hand like a dying friend, sniffling and moaning in grief. Then suddenly he stops.

"What? What the hellrealms?" He says as he looks at his hand, "Who cut me finger!?" He rolls from his fetal position and looks up to see the ladies. "What's going on here? What did ya do with me? Where are we?"

"What?" Sycilia asks. "You don't remember?"

"Remember what?" Noodle says. "Did we?" He raises his eyebrows. "Did we do it?"

"Gross!" Sycilia says.

"That's mean," Noodle says, standing up and holding his hand. "Is that me finger? What did you do?"

"You were being an asshole. So we took your power away."

"I had that?" Noodle points while still holding his fist. "The Ring? I was wearing it?"

"Yeah, and you used it to try and kill us," Recky says. "You also talked to it like it was alive."

"No." Noodle touches his head. "Not the ring. Waller. He talked through that thing."

"You remember?" Sycilia asks.

"I don't remember what I was doing, but I remember the voice. The power. The connection. It overtook me. I was like a puppet."

"Seems convenient," Sycilia says, "You get your ass whooped and then you aren't held accountable for what you did. Look at all these people." With that Recky opens the light shard orb and illuminates the room. Noodle looks around at the bodies.

"Listen lady," Noodle begins, "I didn't do this. In fact, I was probably gonna end up like these people. Shepherd's Flock, it's like a living nightmare. The memories, they are seeping in. I watched these people work themselves to death. They were—we were promised power. These were my men." Noodle bends down and touches a man's body, "this was Gleric Havenstock. He had two boys. Was working for the bandits guild to take care of them."

"Bandit's guild?" Recky asks.

"The most proficient band of muscle you could hire, for all your unscrupulous needs," Noodle says without looking up. He digs into his pocket and with his bloody finger hands a card to Recky, "Take my card. Tell a friend. Best way to help spread the word."

"Why did you come down here? Why are your men dead?" Sycilia pushes.

"Waller. He hired us. When we asked for a deposit, he gave us some onerings, and he promised me a new contract with his boss. That ring, that is not a onering, that's something more. It's a direct connection to The Finger Beast. But like I said, you lose yourself to it."

"How did it affect them?" Sycilia bends down and takes Noodles hand.

"From the thing in the cage," Noodle says.

"Cage?" Sycilia asks.

"This place, it was built to be more than just a place to admire the Sandren. It's a freaking prison. Waller figured he could control the thing that's trapped here, he thought he could use the power of the blade to subdue it."

"So he made these rings, using the power of the Sandren Blade?" Recky asks, grabbing a few rings from the Barrel.

"Careful with those," Sycilia says. "They are extremely powerful. Onerings have a spell charge each, and allow anyone to cast it." She walks over to it and looks at it. "This barrel could bring down Valeward."

"Sounds like a good tool," Recky says.

"It's not. It's too dangerous." Sycilia pulls out her flint and steel and ignites it, launching several sparks onto the wood. "This is the only way to prevent catastrophe." She turns to Noodle.

"How does this blade subdue the monster?"

"Well, first you have to bond to it, like all magic swords."

"Bond?"

"Yeah, you close your eyes, open your mind, and allow it to search you. And when It knows everything about you, then you can access its magic. It's a trade off."

"Teach me how to do it."

"You don't want that," Noodle says.

"Why?"

"Cause bonding forces you to be honest. You have to be honest with yourself and the thing. And I know enough about your past to know that you're compartmentalizing. You've locked things away."

"You don't know me," Sycilia says indignantly.

"I do. That's the thing. I've been bonded to two items now. And I know what it takes. And I don't think you have what it takes."

"Screw you!" Sycilia plops down and holds the sword out.

"Ok," Noodle says. "Now close your eyes and focus

on the dark. Soon you'll see a light, which will become a doorway. You go through that door way and you face what's on the other side. Then,perhaps, you can bond with the thing."

Sycilia breathes in and focuses on the black. Then three words float through her mind, "Hello Rose Petal." And she immediately opens her eyes.

"Nope, uh, uh, nah," Sycilia says standing up and seeing Reacky standing before her. "I'm just gonna have to do that bonding thing later." She looks around, "Where's Noodle?"

"He disappeared, like immediately."

"Really?"

"Like, the second you closed your eyes, he was gone."

"Slippery dick."

Aarik looks up as Gwen approaches. She smiles and runs her hair over her ear. Aarik smiles at her, then directs his eyes to the scene behind her. A table on fire and Elliot staring at Gwen, awe and terror on his face. Aarik stands, ready to go help Elliot.

"What's going on?" Aarik asks.

"I need you to do me a favor and pretend like we're talking," Gwen says.

"Uh, but we are talking."

"Yeah, but like, about something important. Like maybe laugh?"

"Laugh? You want me to laugh?"

"Yeah."

Aarik bellows out and slaps his belly.

"Too much, dude," Gwen hisses. "Now you're making our conversation too interesting." Aarik stops.

"Now put your hand on my shoulder, and invite me

to sit down."

"You realize," Aarik says, "that you're explaining to me what I would be doing if you had just joined me, right?"

"Please," Gwen looks desperate.

Aarik smiles, nods, and puts his hand on her shoulder. As he points to the table and his book, he says, "This is weird, but I'm very interested in learning more about the fire."

"Is it bad? Is Elliot still staring at me?"

"It's bad. He's not paying attention to you at all." Aarik begins his color commentary. "He's looking around for something, and oh, he's just grabbed one of your cauldrons."

"With dinner in it?!"

"No, no, an empty one. And now he's pulling one of our ice blocks out of the wagon. Potsicker is on the table now, in the flames, he's eating something, does Posticker eat flames?"

"No, that's where Elliot put his treats."

"Ah, Elliot sees this and is now shooing away Potsicker, and now Elliot's robe is on fire. He's waving it about, aaaaand now he's on the ground rolling the fire out. He's derobed, and now stands in his scarf and long johns, a good look for him."

"This can't actually be happening, you're making it up."

"Honey, I couldn't make this up if I wanted to," Aarik says. Gwen blushes and runs her hair over her ear again. "Ok, he's taken one of your big butcher knives and is trying to chop the ice. Oh no, ew."

"What?"

"You can say goodbye to that knife. And now he's bleeding pretty bad. He's healed himself. He's good at that. And now he's grabbing that fire wood ax.

Aaaaand, first swing missed."

"Come on," Gwen says, watching Aarik. "You're lying."

"Contact!" Aark says excited. "And the ice shattered. Seems like our little cleric has a bit of muscle behind those spectacles. He's scooping the ice shards into the cauldon now. Oh, and by the way the wagon is on fire."

"No."

"Yes, and he's now noticed, and oooh, that's a bad word, Elliot. Wait, what's this? He's running his hands over the cauldron. Is that magic? He's casting a spell." With this Gwen turns around in time to see Elliot in his gray neck-to-toe long johns, his scarf, and his glowing spectacles, as he cast a spell.

Elliot throws the ice, it glistens in the torch light, gleaming like diamonds. Arcing rainbows and streaming reflections break the air. Elliot throws a burned hand forward and shouts a quick prayer to the universe. His words command the creators of the world into action; It's a plea to the Deities outside the Hallowed Conclave to change the rules of the world.

Each shard of ice breaks, bursts, explodes out, and swirls. Every single ice crystal changes into its own storm. Ice cools the air, forcing the water molecules to chill, causing frost to appear in the sky. Clouds form like a fog and sprinkle down snow. The ice dissipates into a blizzard and covers the flaming carriage and table. It swarms the blaze and extinguishes the fire. Then the clouds themselves harden, take form, and fall from the sky as a final powdery snow, descending on the rest of the camp.

Clapping fills the air as Aarik and Gwen give Elliot a round of applause. "Encore!" Aarik shouts. Potsticker comes out from under the wagon and steps in the snow, melting it immediately. He shakes his butt and begins jumping around in the snow, watching it disappear in his presence.

"Gwen can I have a word with--" Elliot begins, but is cut off.

"Elliot, I did it!" a voice says over him. They all look to see Sycilia making her way from the lake to the camp.

Elliot, covered in fresh fallen snow, looks at Sycilia, beaming in excitement.

"I did it," She says again as she gets closer to him. "What—what happened here?"

"Fire," Elliot says. He shivers and snow falls from his shoulders.

"What happened to your clothes? And your hand?" She asks.

"Fire." Elliot looks down at Potsticker. The creature plays in the snow, looks up with a childish innocence, and Elliot squints at him. Then his face changes to pain, "Owwwie!"

"Your hand is extra crispy," Sycilia says, holding it up.

"Then why are you touching it?" Elliot pulls it back. "I can heal this, It's just gonna take some time. Too many spells in a day."

"Let me bandage it up for you."

'I'm the cleric here, aren't I?"

"You're the damn fool that played with fire," Sycilia says, ripping a piece of her shirt.

"Me?!" He points to Gwen and Aarik who talk over a book, pretending not to watch, "It was, I mean, shes.... It's not my–" Gwen looks up with the same face as Potsticker. Elliot pulls his lips tight and exhales in frustration.

"Burn salve?" Sycilia asks, walking over to the wagon.

"Left chest, under the herbs," Elliot says, sitting at the charred table. "You're back pretty quick. Aarik is usually gone for a whole day. You only really missed lunch."

"That's 'cause I found what I was looking for," Sycilia says, grabbing a bottle from the wagon. She walks back, pouring the salve on the strips of cloth. "We made our way to a chamber in the Underrealm. Have you been there?"

"No," Elliot says.

"Recky and I found a whole nother room with an actual dragon statue, and it was filled with dead bodies"

"What?" Elliot's eyes light up.

"I thought that'd get your attention." Sycilia laughs. She begins to apply the bandages, Elliot hisses. She gives him a look of irritation. "They hadn't been dead long, and their eyes had been melted," She continues, "Something had taken control of their minds and sucked their energy."

"An aberrant?"

"Maybe, but while we were down there, we found something else."

"What is it?"

"Noodle."

"Noodle?

"Yeah."

"Noodle the elf?"

"You know how I've been investigating the onerings? The only thing I had was a name, Waller. I had nothing else to go off of. How did they make the onerings, who is Waller, where is he?"

"Yeah,"

"Well now I have this." She pulls out of her sheath a sword, a new blade, and lets it shine in the light.

The blade is black, in fact the majority of the sword is black. The handguard laid with gold, black leather wraps around the hilt and the pommel is an uncut gem.

"Is that a magic blade?"

"Not just any magic blade," Sycilia says.

"Thats the Sandren Blade!" Aarik screams from the far table. He jumps over his place and runs as fast as he can to see the item in Sycilia's possession. "You found the Sandren Blade. You have the Sandren Blade, you, you, you stole it from me!"

"I didn't," Sycilia saysm pulling it away from his sight.

"I've spent weeks looking for that thing in these tunnels, and then the one time you head out for a morning hike, you just stumble on it?"

"Yeah, so?"

"So...." Aarik stops for a second, thinking about the situation. He then devolves. "So, I want it!"

"No, it's mine."

"But I put all this work into it, I should get it."

"I found it. It chose me."

"It chose you? Chose you? Can you believe this?" Aarik turns to Elliot, who watches them squabble. "Tell her she has to give it to me."

"Don't bring him into this."

"You're her boss. She has to do what you say."

"Stop it, you're not getting the sword."

"Do you even understand what you have in your hands? That's the sword of the last dragon king of Yonder Valley. The blade he used to strike down the darkness of the land. The blade of the dracoelves."

"The dracoelves?" Sycilia asks.

"How do you know about all that?" Elliot asks.

"I read it in your book," Aarik says to Elliot, then

turns to Sycilia. "'Cause I can actually read."

"Screw you, I can read!"

"See Jane swing a sword." Aarik picks on her, "See Jane kill a bandit. That is barely reading."

"Which book did you read it in?" Elliot asks.

"That one, with Gwen," Aarik says. He points to the book on the table he was just at. "Plus, we know that that book was mostly pictures," Aarik continues while Elliot focuses on Gwen reading the book at Aarik's table.

"Let me just hold it," Aarik says, as Elliot walks away from the argument.

"No, you don't get to make fun of me and demand my stuff."

"Sharing is caring, Sycilia, remember what mom taught you?"

"Remember when mom taught you boundaries?"

"I remember mom talking about boundaries, and how I learned they don't apply to me."

"Reading about dracoelves?" Elliot asks, standing over Gwen. She looks up sheepishly.

"Somehow they're the key to opening that door of yours," Gwen says.

"Do you know why?" Elliot asks, sitting down, his face stone still, eye unyielding.

"I haven't gotten to that part yet, I guess," Gwen says looking down at the page. A drawing of the Sandren Blade is on the parchment.

"That's ok, I have. I've read through that thing several times. I know what it's missing," Elliot says. He puts his hand out over the book and turns several pages. When he finds the right one, he leaves it open and watches as she reads it.

Elliot's eyebrow cocks upward, and he adjusts his glasses. "You know where we could get some?"

"Please, don't," Gwen says.

"Don't what? I'm just asking someone who can hold a ball of living fire, where we can get—"

"Please," She looks up, tears filling her eyes.

"So what do you think?" Aarik shouts at Elliot. "We gonna try this thing?" Elliot turns around and looks at the twins. He gets up and walks so that they can't see Gwen tearing up.

"Sycillia, what does that have to do with Waller and the onerings?" Elliot says as he walks back.

"Oh, yeah, the best part," she says. "When we were down there, this room was littered with dead bodies. Fresh, dead bodies."

"That's the best part?" Aarik asks.

"Shh, they were all wearing the onerings on their hands. And this blade was in the mouth of a dragon statue, and more rings were sitting on the teeth of the dragon, and there was a barrel filled with onerings. He was using this to power the onerings."

"This was the power source for all those rings?" Elliot asks.

"The blade is said to capture spells and then reuse them," Aarik says. "Do you think he was using the sword to inject those spells into the rings?"

"Noodle, who was under some brainwashing spell from his own ring, ended up doing some ritual to help Waller gain control of the darkness that the Sandren locked away in this temple." She holds the blade up "And this is the key."

"The Sandren locked the aberrant in this place?" Gwen asks.

"Not just somewhere." Sycilia smiles.

"Behind the door," Elliot says.

They all look at the massive door built into the Sandren's legs.

"Makes sense," Aarik says. "This place is like a fortress, and the dracoelves would have spent their lives guarding the door, making sure the thing behind there is contained."

"But with this sword," Sycilia says, "I can do it. I can finish off the monster, and stop Waller."

"No," Elliot says. He rubs his head, and looks away from the door, "No, we don't open that door."

"What? Why?" Sycilia protests.

"If that really is where the aberrant is, then we need to get help here before we open it."

"Come on, Elliot," Sycilia says. "Let me do this, then you get to open the door and see what else is behind it."

"The answer is no, Sycilia. I'm sorry. Truly. I wanted to open that door as much, if not more, than anyone. But I won't put this place at risk for my curiosity." With that Elliot takes his book, looking at Gwen, and walks back to his tent.

Sycilia holds her blade, watching the waterfalls surrounding the statue of the Sandren. She closes her eyes and listens to the water roaring, and a soft light splits the dark behind her eyes. She then hears a whisper. "Hello, Rose Petal."

"So we're like, one hundred percent going to open that tonight, right?" Aarik whispers, breaking her from the whisper in her mind. Sycilia lets a sly smile crawl across her face.

The lake in front of the dragon king statue is majestic. Most lights in the air have been snuffed and the small pop up town is quiet. The boat disturbs the tranquil water of the lake, splashing and rocking back and forth. Behind them, the tent city is asleep, most of the lights snuffed out.

"Ok, I'll hold it while you row," Aarik says.

"What? No, it's mine, stop trying to steal it."

"So you expect me to row? Not happening, lady. You're the one that wants to get to that door so bad. I'm just protecting you."

"Protecting me? I have a magic sword!"

"Have you bonded to it yet?" Aarik asks. This takes Sycilia off guard.

"Bonded? Yeah. Yes. I have."

"No you haven't, you liar. Do you even know how?"

"Noodle told me how, and then he ran away, so I'll get to it later."

"After you row us over there," Aarik says.

"Hey!" A hiss comes from the banks of the lake. Elliot and Gwen stand at the edge of the water, "What are you two doing?"

"We're gonna go open the door," Sycilia hisses back.

"What?!" Elliot shouts as a scream, "No, come back and we'll deal with this in the morning."

"If Waller is in there then we need to go now," Sycilia pleads.

"If he's in there, then he's trapped in there. A few more hours won't change that. Come back and we can do this later."

"I'm sorry Elliot, but no." Sycilia grabs the oars and rows.

"No, no, you don't," Elliot says frustrated. "You get back here!" Elliot gets in a boat and rows. Gwen, carrying Potsticker and a lantern, gets in the boat. "No, you're not coming,"

"I'm not getting out," Gwen says. "And they're going to get away."

"DERN IT! DERN IT TO HECK!" Elliot whispers.

Two row boats set out on the small lake, lit by the

bioluminescent mushrooms on the walls of the temple, Potstickers light, and a torch in Aarik's hands. Moving across the black waters, trying to out pace the other.

"This is a nice night," Aarik says.

"Shut up," Sycilia says.

"Why do you want to get in there so bad? Don't get me wrong, I want it too, but only 'cause I want to see this baby in action," Aarik says as he touches the blade with his toe.

"I just do," she rows on.

"Come on," Aarik puts his hand on Sycilia's hand stopping her from rowing.

"He's gonna catch up."

"You're really worried about that?" Aarik asks, turning around to watch Elliot. Elliot huffs and puffs, stopping every few strokes to adjust his glasses.

"I'm coming! You're not leaving me behind," Elliot says.

"Yeah, we got some time," Sycilia says.

"What's going on?"

"I want to find out what's behind that door. Same as Elliot."

"No, it's something else."

"This is the first break in the onering...ring. I can't let it slip by."

"It's not going to."

"It might, though. And I need to prove that I can do my job. And I need to prove that I don't need anyone else. I don't need people holding my hand all the time."

"You're bringing me."

"You don't count."

"Ouch."

"No, Aarik, you know what I mean. You're my brother, you're a part of me. I just, I haven't done anything significant without Elliot, Ella, or Moses. I feel so useless."

"I get it."

"No you don't," she says, annoyed.

"I do. Compared to you I'm a tag along. You were the one that pushed Elliot to get the Penny Lich. You helped take down the main onering...ring. Gah that's clunky. Onering group?

"Onering cell?" Sycilia adds.

"Onering Cabal?"

"I like that. It has a nice ominous ring to it."

Gwen shouts, "The onering band."

"Oh, that's good," Aarik shouts back. "Thank you, Gwen." Elliot continues to huff and puff as Sycilia smirks. "You guys move at all in the last minute?"

"I think the current pushed us back closer to the edge," Gwen says.

"Oh, come on," Elliot grunts.

"You and Moses took care of the onering band in Valeward. You and Ella fought a creature that's been plaguing the Thickstem Village for generations. I've gotten drunk and slept with a bunch of people. But it is a lot of people. Like so many people."

"I know, the walls are thin in our apartment."

"Those are only the ones I bring home. There's so many more. You have no idea."

"Gross."

"The point is, just 'cause you don't accomplish anything on your own, doesn't mean you haven't accomplished something." Aarik takes the oars and begins rowing, "It might be a good idea to start bonding with that blade."

Gwen reaches into her satchel and pulls out a small

vial of blood. "Here," she says, handing it to Elliot. He stops rowing and looks at it.

"What is it?" he grabs it.

Gwen stretches her lips with her tongue, and looks away. "It's my blood." Elliot looks at it, then looks at her hand, a bandage wrapped around it.

"So you, you're—"Yes."

"And you're giving me this? Why?"

"Because you were right about me and Aarik, and I appreciate you pushing me to talk to him. You're someone I think I can trust. I hope you'll see that I trust you, and you won't do something stupid, like tell people."

"Would you be willing to let me see?" Elliot asks, putting the vial in his robe inside pocket. Gwen shakes her head.

"I can't just turn it off, that's not how the glimmers work. They last until they last." Gwen looks ashamed.

"Look, I'm not asking to be, like a weirdo or something, and if your answer is no, then so be it. I understand the weight of this. I appreciate the gravity of the situation. I have been reading about things in books my entire life, and I have recently begun to see them come to life. The Sandren Temple? Do you have any idea how long I've wanted to come here?"

"I know, But I seriously can't drop it, and—"

"That's fine, don't worry about it," Elliot says. "Can I ask, though, why me? Why not, you know, Aarik? Or Sycilia?"

Gwen looks past Elliot to the other two, "Do you know much about dragons?"

"Yeah," Elliot says, then realizes how he sounds. "I mean, I know a bit, sure."

"They could shape change. They could be whatever they needed to be in order to find a mate."

"Sure, that's why the Sandren is the Sandren and not him or her. Still don't understand why they named them king. I guess there's no nonbinary version of monarch."

"Monarch is nonbinary."

"Hooo, shit."

"They were a king because in elven tradition, the male was the head of the family and estate. When it came to monarchs, the family was the royal family and the estate was the kingdom." Gwen shifts in her seat. "When there was no male authority in a household, the woman was incharge of the estate, but the head of the family was always a male. An uncle, cousin, grandfather. The men always watched over their family. So when they proclaimed the Sandren ing, they were saying that the dragon was head of both the kingdom and the royal family. It was his job to propagate the elves of Yonder Valley. When he chose Mother Mable as his queen, they created the dracoelves."

"I know all this. I'm waiting for you to answer the question," Elliot says, dropping the oars. "The Sandren could take the form of a man, and they did, seeing as Mother Mable was female. But the children, the dracoelves, could not choose what form they wanted. They were forced to live life as genderless beings. They did not reproduce, they were born directly through the union of the dragon and the fey ancestry."

"So you aren't truly a...."

"I am what I know I am. And I have found ways to be what I am."

"But like, physically, you're—"

"Not what someone like Aarik would want to be with. I can't tell him because he would look at me differently. I would rather lie to the world, and have them engage with me, than be honest and feel their pity, remorse, or hatred."

"So why me?" Elliot says with the same concern and sincerity he had earlier.

"Cause you don't care about that. You're a cleric, you can't have sex, so it doesn't change your thoughts on people. And because, you're, I dunno, you're you. I can see the good in your eyes, and I've seen the way you treat people. You're a good soul. It's the same reason Aster chose you." She holds up Potsticker.

"He's gonna love that you can hold him."

"Dragon ancestry baby!" Gwen says in a soft yell. "Fire resistance comes in handy in the kitchen."

"Do you feel anything yet?" Aarik asks.

"Shut up," Sycilia says as she sits holding the sword horizontally. The blade in one hand, while the hilt rests in another. Her legs are crossed, and behind her is the overbearing statue of the Sandren.

"You need to focus on the blade. Let the way it feels become a part of how you feel." Aarik rows the boat and watches her. "You need to block out everything, leave this world and let the magic of the blade replace the air around you. Breathe in its essence and force out all distractions–"

"Like you talking?" Sycilia opens one eye. Aarik gives her silent attitude, zipping his mouth shut and watching her. She closes her eyes again, feeling the rowing of the boat, the lapping of water. The sound of the massive cave around them. She can feel the blade vibrating in her hand.

Then a small pin prick of light begins to open up in her sight. The darkness in her mind gives way to a sliver of white. It grows in her mind, and she can feel the sword cutting through the black upward. Then left, then down. The shape of a door sits in her mind.

She walks toward it, puts her hand on it, and pushes forward. The door opens and the bright light over
takes her.

Her eye's adjust and she can see a figure standing in
the room.

"Hello, Rose Petal," the figure says in a soft but deep
voice. Sycilia immediately opens her eyes.

"Nope, still not ready for that."

"Not ready for what?" Aarik asks.

"To bond with something."

"Is this about, mister you know who?"

"It's about bonding."

"You're bonded to me," Aarik says as he finishes
pulling up to the stone platform in front of the door.

"Again, you don't count."

"Again... ouch." Aarik turns around to see that Elliot
and Gwen float directionless in the water. Sycilia steps
out of the boat and pulls it to the platform, tying it
down. Aarik steps on the stone and looks up at the
building sized door before him. He then turns back to
Elliot.

"You guys gonna come?"

"The current is too strong," Elliot says.

"Are you serious?" Sycilia laughs.

The smell of atmosphere, and a rool of thunder claps
around Sycilia, Aarik summons his bow, nocks an
arrow, and aims it at Elliot.

"Hey man," Elliot says, "whatcha doing?

Aarik releases the arrow, it flies toward Elliot, a metal wire attached to it. The blade sinks into the front of
the boat and Aarik begins to pull it in. Sycilia grabs on
and helps. Within a minute the Cleric's boat arrives at
the platform of the door.

"Thanks," Elliot says. "I figured we'd be floating out
there for a while."

"You need to work out," Aarik says. "When we get back to the Penny Lich, I'm putting you through boot camp."

"Sounds good," Elliot says. "As long as we don't have to get up too early."

Aarik looks irritated.

"Or change my diet, I have a strict clerical diet," Elliots continues. "And I'm adverse to cardio, as my lungs give out quite easily."

"You know what? Nevermind," Aarik says.

Slink! The sound of blade on stone echos. Sycilia slides the blackened blade into a port in the wall.

"Here we go! Time to find out what's hiding behind door number one."

A moment passes, nothing changes, the cave flows with water from above.

"Any second now, right?" Sycilia says. She waits, then tries the blade again. "What the hells? This is the key, right?"

"This might help," Elliot says, pulling the vial of blood from his pocket.

"What's that?" Aarik asks.

"Blood of a dracoelf."

"What?" Sycilia asks.

"The dracoelves were a race of people created from the union of the Sandren and Mother Mable," Elliot says. "The door can only be opened when one with the dragon's bloodline is present to open it." He walks over to the spot where the sword cuts into the wall, opens the vial and pours it on his hand. He then places the bloody hand print in a square on the door. The stone absorbs the blood mark left behind.

The sword turns like a key, and the sudden rumble of the opening door trembles through the cavern. The stone moves to either side of the doorway, sliding left and right. The waterfalls are blocked off and stop. The lake calms, and there are only gentle ripples from the earthquake.

Out of the black, a hand breaks out and grabs the left side of the doorway. A second hand slithers its way out of the dark, grasping the other side The hands, as big as houses, crunch the portal rim, breaking the stone they hold onto.

A roar emanates from the darkness, and the black hands pull a body forward. Black inky tentacles writhe outward, wiping and feeling the air. Some attach to the doorway as the body of the creature appears.

The tentacles race back to the neck of the massive beast, as they coalesce together. The neck runs down to a lean and tall body. Blackened and dark like ink, sweating slime, screaming out in angered agony. The Finger Beast emerges.

"I don't think you should have opened that door," Gwen says.

"You know what?" Elliot says, staring at the emerging horror of unknown understanding. "I say we talk to it and see what it wants."

A sudden bolt of light arcs through the sky. A monk stands at the banks of the lake, magic ring aglow from the spell he cast. The monk stands defiant and ready to take the creature down...hen his ring radiates dark energy.

A strand of black magic wiggles its way from his hand and shoots toward the great eldritch monster. The titans's black tentacle head shoots out a single strand connecting to the ring.

The monk goes limp, and his eyes turn back in his head. He then snaps back and growls, staring at Sycilia holding the blade.

"You gonna ask him, too?" Gwen asks.

"But he's all the way over there," Elliot says.

The monk dives into the lake and swims toward the party, the black tendril holding onto him.

Several more blasts of elemental magic streak the air and strike the monster. Its body reacts with the joys of pain, rippling in agony, then quickly releases its head tendrils toward the monks and dwarves using their magic rings.

"Are they using onerings?" Sycilia asks.

"It looks like it," Aarik says. "How do they all have them?"

"Recky," Sycilia says.

"Recky?" Elliot asks.

"When we found the Sandren Blade it was being used to enchant the rings. There was a whole barrel of onerings. She must have taken some before I burned them to the ground."

"Why is she giving the rings to people?" Elliot asks.

"Seriously?" Aarik points up to the monster now standing below the statue of the Sandren, both towering over the encampment. "There's a freaking shadow demon coming out of the door you just opened. It makes perfect sense."

"Aarik's right," Sycilia says. "If I hadn't known what the onerings were, I probably would have grabbed them. They're very useful for..." Several more blasts of magic launch into the air and hit the monster. "...well, that."

As soon as the magic is used up in the rings, each one begins to radiate dark energy. The same tendrils stream out of the rings and fly upward, connecting to the monster's head. Each user is hit and taken over by the dark magic of the massive beast. Their bodies go limp, eyes roll back, and then they snap back to life with hatred. All of them begin swimming toward the altar where the four heroes stand.

"The problem is, it looks like everytime they use the rings, this monster takes them over," Elliot says.

"Just like Noodle," Sycilia says. "He had a ring, a magic one. Said his new employer gave it to him, but it took over his mind."

"He told you this?" Elliot asks.

"Yeah, after I cut his finger off and he regained his freewill." Sycilia pulls the finger still wearing the ring out of her pocket.

"You've been carrying that around this whole time!?" Elliot gags.

"These are the sorta details you tell people when you come back from the dungeon delve," Aarik says, looking at the finger.

"I wanted to do some more research and track down the maker of these things."

"Waller?" Elliot asks.

"Yeah," Sycilia says with guilt.

"Well, here's the problem," Aarik slips the ring off the detached finger and holds the rings up. "The outside of the ring has the spell infused." Aarik shows Elliot the inside. "But the inside has a curse. As soon as the magic is used, the curse takes hold of the user's mind."

"This thing's taking control of their minds?" Elliot asks.

"Hey, I hate to interrupt the lesson," Gwen says, "but that monster is towering over us, and those mind controlled people are getting close."

"I've got just what we need!" Elliot shouts.

"Is it a wand of spells? Fireball in a jar?" Aarik looks too excited, then looks up at the gargantuan shadow, its leg going up to step on them.

"Chalk!" Elliot says, pulling a stick of chalk out of his

sleeve.

"Chalk?!" They all scream. But within a flash Elliot draws a quick magic sigil around him.

"Everyone hold on," They crowd around him, and Potsticker grabs onto the back of Elliot's shirt with his mouth.

Poof!

In the split second before the monster's foot landed on them, they vanished into thin air. At that exact same moment, over at their camp, Elliot, Sycilia, Aarik, Gwen, and Potstciker all burst back into existence.

They all throw up, including Potstickers lava like spew.

"That was my first time with dimension shifting. Funny enough it's a simplified version of telep–"

"Shut up." Sycilia picks Elliot up. "We have to go. The exit is right--"

CRASH! Crumble, rumble, broken.

The dark colossus had ripped the hand off the Sandren statue and thrown it. The massive rock had floated through the air and smashed into the wall with the exit door. The exit was gone, the columns destroyed... again.

"Hey look at that," Aarik says. "Now we don't have to run."

The minions of the creature turn and advance toward them all, while the great beast marches through the water.

Sycilia stands sturdy and resolute. Her blade on her shoulder. "Hey, so this thing." She points to her blade. "It's magic cause it can store a spell, right? That's like it's thing?"

"From the lore, yeah," Elliot says. She throws it on the ground near them, kicks a man back in water and throws another over herself. Aarik gets up and begins shooting, pinning men down by their feet. "Mind juicing me up?" Sycilia turns and focuses on the fight, and in that moment Gwen touches the blade. Fire erupts from her hand and she can feel her magic begin to drain from her body. The sword takes all she gives, and she feels for the first time, relieved, light. She smiles at Elliot and kicks the blade back to Sycilia.

"There ya go!" Gwen says.

"Thanks, Elliot!" Sycilia says. "I owe you a drink." She takes the blade and begins swinging it around. It's hot blade simmering in the air. Then she runs up a staircase in the walls of the temple.

"Where are you going?" Aarik shouts.

"To get a better angle!" Sycilia shouts back. "Distract it for me!"

Aarik sinks several arrows in the monster's body, each one with a thin metallic string attached to it, all leading back to Aarik. The dark giant moves toward them, legs still in the water. It bends over, "If this works, I owe you a drink Ella," Aarik says. He then moves his hands in a ritual and speaks a few soft words, but as he speaks his voice distorts with the sound of power, of pure energy. From his hands a great flash of lightning shoots out, and he holds the metal wires in a firm grip. The electricity moves instantaneously up the wires and jolts into the titan. Its body convulses and lumbers backward, smashing into the rock backdrop. Only a few moments pass as the giant tentacle-headed beast walks back into the lake. Its tendrils hold firm to the monks and the Ironhide dwarves. They clamor and slip out of the lake, looking for the small party who opened the door.

"Elliot," Aarik says, getting up close and whispering to the cleric, "You have to do another teleportation spell."

"I'm so tired, and I can't just do that. That was a small spell, you're asking for a big teleport here."

"Look bud," Aarik says, "I get it, you're tired as hell, magic takes it out of you, it takes everything you have. I understand. But right now, if you don't do this? We're screwed. You understand? Sycilia and Gwen are dead. Potsticker is dead. And most importantly, you know who you'd be letting down?"

"Me, I'd be letting myself down," Elliot says, agreeing.

"No, screw that," Aarik says. "You'd be letting me down, Do you understand how dark this world would be if I died? It's your job to get me out of these situations. It's why I stick around. That and the pretty boys and girls."

"Fine, Fine." Elliot says, "I'll do it, but you all have to keep those things away from me. I can't focus if I'm being attacked."

"Done," Aarik says, whistling for Potsticker to tag along with him.

"Let's get to work Gwen. This one is going to be extremely complicated."

"Why me?" Gwen says.

"Because if you really are a dracoelf, there is magic inside you. And I need all the help I can get, I'm almost tapped out here."

"I don't think I can—"

"Can I trust you?" Elliot offers her the chalk. She looks at it, clicks her tongue and nods.

Taking the chalk, she says, "Yeah, let's do this."

"Potsticker!" Aarik shouts as The Finger Beast begins to move toward the lake shore. "You keep that molester monster in the water." Potsticker runs through the crowd and quickly begins unleashing lava vomit into the water.

Sycilia runs forward and shoulder checks a monk, kicks over a dwarf, and slams her hilt into another man. A man comes raging toward Sycilia, and she ducks under his attack, forcing him over her body. Two more come from the stairs. The first she perries with her blade, and the second stops as a dagger sinks into his leg. He doubles over in agony, shouting, "Give us the sword! I'll let you live, you can leave, just leave me the blade of the Sandren."

Sycilia looks over the balcony, preparing for a leap. "Sandren Blade belongs to me."

"You fool!" Voices from the fog filter through, "You have no idea the power in the blade. You will never know." Fog rolls over the banks of the lake, as Potst-ciker evaporates the water. Through it the flames of Potsticker can be seen barely holding off the monster.

"We need to go," Aarik says. "Now!" He whistles. Potsticker turns at the whistle and begins running as quickly as his little nubs can take him.

"It better be ready!" Aarik shouts as they arrive back at the circle. He looks down to see pieces missing from the sigils being drawn. "Are you two kidding me! Those arcane sigils haven't even been defined!"

"Aarik, please," Gwen says, working on the runes for her part of the ritual. Aarik gets down real close to the line and stares at it,

"This wayline has yet to be charged. You're not even charging as you lay it down?"

"Aarik, if you know so much about this spell, then help us," Elliot says, adjusting his glasses.

"I can't, I...I have to help Sycilia fight off the mob."

"Potsticker is kinda handling that," Gwen says. Pot-sticker burns the tents and shacks, creating a wall of debris and flame.

"I have to, uh. Help, Sycilia fight that monster." He begins to run, then stops.

Aarik looks back to the ritual circle. Gwen holds up a piece of chalk.

"Hurry," Gwen says. Aarik looks at the chalk, and then he takes in the sight of the magic circle and the dire situation. He breathes quickly and tears begin to form. His shaky hand reaches out, and he takes the limestone stick.

Aarik drops down and shows Gwen the lines he intends and begins speaking words to charge the sigil as he draws. Elliot follows and does the same. He hands the spell book to Gwen, and she begins to direct their drawing.

The creature's head wiggles only a few feet below Sycilia. She breathes in heavily and rocks back and forth, contemplating the drop and point of attack. She readies her blade.

"You're not ready," a voice says from behind her. She spins around in terror, ready to attack. Noodle leans against the wall, holding a piece of fruit.

"What the flapjack are you doing here?!" she hisses.

"I'm paying you back."

"Is that a threat?" She readies herself again.

"Chill out," Noodle says, taking a bite of his food. "You saved my life, missy. By chopping this old ring finger off, you saved me from a life of servitude and tireless dedication to a single entity. Marriage was never in my plans and now I'm free of that prick. So I owe you."

"You gonna help me attack that thing?"

"Are you insane? No, I'm gonna help you realize how to really use that thing." He points to the sword. "That blade is powerful beyond your comprehension. The reason he wants it so bad."

"Yeah, I kinda figured that. That's why I'm gonna take it and stick it inside that monster."

"But it doesn't work for you, not the way you want it to." The elf walks over to the edge. "It's the same way gravity works. Lots of people know how to use it to help them walk, or jump or move about, but they don't control it. You got gravity in the blade, girly. You need to open up to it so it can open up to you.

"What are you saying?"

"I saw you earlier. You started to bond with the blade."

"So?"

"So, why didn't ya?"

"I didn't feel like it."

"Mmhmm. Sure. I think ya scared, girly."

"I'm not scared."

"I've done this before, ya know. With the Blade of Mable. I bonded to it. Opened myself up to it. I learned its secrets, and it learned mine. My deepest darkest fears. That's how magic works: it's being honest with reality, so that you can lie to the world around you."

"So what? I'm supposed to just sit here and meditate while my friends die?"

"That little flame thing seems to be holding his ground for a moment," Noodle says as he walks away. "Just a bit of advice, I wouldn't let whoever it is talk too much, I'd just kill 'em and get it over with."

"Where are you going?" Sycilia asks.

"To find a new boss," Noodle says, then with the snap of his finger he vanishes from sight.

"When did Noodle get cool?" Sycilia asks. She then looks down at her blade, closes her eyes, and breathes in deep. The door of light cuts out of the darkness of her mind and she stands ready to open it.

"I'm done!" Aarik shouts. He looks up in time to see a burning man running from Potsticker's flames. He runs for the group, but Aarik quickly summons his bow, taking an arrow out at the same time, and releases an arrow into the man's chest. He stops and falls.

"Elliot," he says.

"I'm double checking the sigils."

"We don't have time for that," Aarik says.

"We do. We can't leave without Sycilia. And I have to check the composition of velocities."

"I introduced that expression here," Aarik says.

"Oh...I see.... Well done," Elliot says. "That's quite, well, that's impressive."

"Thanks." He shoots another charger.

"It's wrong, but still quite good."

"Wrong?" Aarik looks down.

"See, the static field is represented in the kinematics, when it should be a part of the metric signature of the time dilation," Elliot says as he fixes the lines and symbols.

"Oh, my Divine," Aarik says. His stare is distant. His body is rigid.

"With that calculation we would have been...."

"Blown to pieces, ripped from the fabric of reality," Aarik cuts Elliot off. Elliot looks up and sees tears in Aarik's eyes.

"Possibly," Elliot stands up and puts his hand on Aarik's shoulder. "But also," he looks at the sigil, then adjusts his glasses and nods his head left to right weighing the expression, "we could have been thrown into another form of reality. Another universe. We wouldn't be here, but we'd still be alive."

Aarik shakes his head and he comes to terms with

what Elliot says. "Wait, we could have survived?"

"Guys," Gwen says, pointing at the mob. They collect water from the lake and use it to create a path through the flames. Potsticker, for all his efforts, looks worn out, huffing and puffing to create more flame.

"It's moving!" Gwen shouts, as Elliot and Aarik stand next to her looking at the army of minions approaching, while the massive blackened tentacle monster begins walking toward them.

It reaches its hand out and seems to stretch its limbs to reach them.

"We have to go," Gwen says.

In unison the boys say, "Not without Sycilia."

Elliot whistles, Potsticker turns back and joins them, running from the encroaching blackness that begins to overtake the camp. The glowing rings peering out from the darkness and smoke.

"Guys.... We have to–" Gwen begins, but is cut off as she sees a streak of light cut the dark figure.

Sycilia, with a flaming sword, jumps from the fourth story balcony, aiming the blade for the chest of the monster.

At once the minions turn back to see her. They begin to scramble as she slices through the flesh of The Finger Beast. She holds on tight and digs the sword in as she comes to a stop halfway down the belly of the beast.

Black ichor spews out from the creature's wound and a roar of wretchedness spits out. The minions mimic the pain and scream. While still screaming, they run to the monster and climb up its legs.

Sycilia speaks a forceful spell. Her eyes glow and then she turns and plants her feet on the titan while holding the blade.

The blade glows brightly inside the dark body of

the creature. It burns and begins to simmer the flesh.
With the last word of the spell, Sycilia forces the blade
in another foot and ignites the great eldritch thing
from inside.

Its body explodes and pushes Sycila away, sailing
though the air and unconscious. The minions fall to
the ground like leaves from a tree. The blackness of
the creature splits and reveals a plant-like thing, with
tentacles whipping about.

The dark tendrils flicker, looking for the rings to
reestablish control over the minions.

Elliot and Aarik both race forward. Aarik out paces
Elliot, sliding next to where his sister lands and checking her pulse.

"She's alive!" Aarik shouts.

"Behind you!" Elliot's shouts. Aarik looks back in
time to see several tendrils streaking toward him.
He reached for the Sandren Blade and lifts it just in
time to slice them. The monster screams and pulls the
limbs back to itself.

"She's fading," Elliot says, hand on Sycilia's neck.
"She hit the ground hard, and she's been burned badly."

"Can you fix it?" Aarik asks. He then turns and slices
at the next attack.

"I...I'm losing energy, Aarik. I don't know if I can
heal her and teleport us."

"Elliot, come on man, you gotta do something. Look
at her!"

"Go...." Sycilia gurgles. "Save your pretty face." She
then passes out. Elliot looks over to Gwen, who is still
watching from the ritual circle. The cleric grimaces
and stretches his neck in irritation.

"Conclave, help me," Elliot says then follows with a
prayer over the woman. Aarik watches as light passes

from Elliot's eyes through his body, then hands, and then seeps into Sycilia. The burns on her legs heal, the swelling on her face goes down, and the look of suffering fades into that of peace.

Aarik looks up to see Elliot finish the spell, then begin to fall. Aarik rushes over and catches Elliot.

"I'm spent, Aarik. She was on the verge of death. It took all of my strength to bring her back."

"So no teleport?"

"No teleport."

"Dern it to heck!!" Aarik shouts. Several tentacles whip past him. He ducks and dodges, then props Elliot over his shoulder, grabs Sicilia's collar and pulls them both to the ritual circle.

Several minions, after being hit with the tentacles again, stand and rush toward the party. Aarik pulls his bow in, and Potsticker unleashes one last blast of fire to surround them. Just as the flames take to the air, a final whipping tentacle finds its way to Aarik and stabs through his back. He doubles over, dropping Sycilia and Elliot. Sycilia grunts as she lays unconscious. Elliot is exhausted, to the point of delusion. Aarik now writhes in pain.

Gwen holds the spell book and watches the mob encircling them outside of the fire. The tentacles of the monster writhe about in the distance.

"Where was this teleport going to take us?" Aarik asks as he drinks a potion.

"The only place I know that has a working teleportation sigil," Elliot says.

"I hope they have good food there," Aarik says as he passes out.

"Gwen," Elliot says weakly, "cast it."

"What? I can't! I don't know anything about time space dilation and stuff."

"You don't have to, I did all the math for you. You can trust it, just say the words and believe in your power."

"Elliot, I can't,"

"You have to."

Potsticker lets out one last feeble blast of fire, then falls on Elliot in exhaustion.

"Do it," Elliot says.

Gwen looks down at the book. She takes one last second, then begins. Her words flow from a place within her that she kept quiet—he part of her soul that lay dormant, waiting to show its power. Waiting to be seen.

"You look so freaking cool right now," Elliot says.

Gwen opens their eyes and sees that their skin has changed to a golden scale pattern. The scales shimmer in the fire's light, leaner, more defined muscles protrude from below. On her neck, the scales are elongated and metallic.

"Hold on, darling," Gwen says, their voice slightly deeper now, eyes shining.

Within a flash, all of time and reality warp. The space around them spins on in the universe as they are left behind in their circle. The moment they are completely detached from the universe, they are flung back into it with tethers binding them to a new location. And a new warp in gravity.

Then in a blink of an eye they are surrounded by bored looking, old, hooded figures. They stand at desks piled with books, and the lights are candles overlooking the pages of history, magic, and lore.

Before a heart beats fully, the party teleports to the Candle Crypts.

"I told you guys I was gonna come back as a big time adventurer," Elliot says before passing out. The hooded figures look surprised for only a moment before one of them runs forward and begins helping.

Gwen grabs Potsicker. "Careful of him," they say as they back away. "He'll melt your skin off your bones."

The Penny Lich in Haberdashery Woods is quite different from the one in Valeward. The biggest difference is that the Haberdashery Woods Penny Lich is owned and operated by a family of goblins.

"Goblins," Noodle whispers to himself in disgust. "When did they become civilized?" He sits at a booth watching the staff walk about. Their light green skin and dark green hair were the most striking difference in anatomy.

Noodle takes a sip of his drink and grimaces at the strength of the spirit. Then breathes out in surprise with the alcohol fuming out of his mouth.

"'Scuse me!" He waves a goblin server down. She is pretty despite her yellow eyes and rounded mouth. When she smiles, Noodle can see the fangs hidden behind her lips.

"Yes?"

"What is this drink? It's fantastic."

"It's our house special. We make it in the basement."

"You make it here?"

"Yes, sir. The Ragamuffin Moonshine. Would you like to tour our distillery?"

"I would, but I'm meeting someone here. Maybe you could send two more of these my way?"

"You got it sir." The goblin girl walks off, and Noodle talks to his drink quietly.

"Gotta say, these goblins ain't half bad."

"Well I'm glad to see they won you over, Noodle," a voice says from above. Noodle looks up to see the Mistress. She coolly sits down and Noodle smiles.

"I suppose I owe you a bit of gratitude," the mistress says.

"Well, I'll take it in the form of a drink then." With that, the goblin girl puts two drinks on the table. The Mistress attempts to take her drink when Noodle slowly takes both to his side of the table. "Oh, these are both for me." He takes a sip of his second drink. "Did you want something?"

"No," the Mistress says, amused. "I will have to go back to Valeward soon. I've been gone for too long as it is."

"So you got into the temple then?"

"We did, and we found what you described: the bodies, the dead monster, the ravaged temple of the Sandren. But we didn't find anyone from the Penny Lich Guild."

"No?" Noodle sips on his drink. "Guess they're more capable than I thought. And The Finger Beast?"

"Dead," the Mistress says. "But from our estimates, Noodle, this one was a spawn, only born the moment the door opened. Do you have any more information on what Waller was planning?"

"He only told me what to do, not what his plan was." Noodle taps his head, "He didn't see me as important enough to confide in."

"Well, It seems you've done your work, and put yourself at great risk for the sake of this realm once again. Grimander Inc., thanks you."

"Yeah? Thanks are nice and all, but you know what I want, Mistress."

"I do indeed."

"So?"

"There is a plan in place," the Mistress says. Noodle rolls his eyes in irritation. "And we believe it's time to make you a field manager."

"Does this mean I get...." "Indeed. You get to meet him, officially."

"Well, well, well." Noodle smiles. He scoots the third drink in front of him toward the mistress. "Looks like we really do have something to share a drink over now."

After getting a degree in film and media, T.W. Clawson realized that he didn't want to make movies, he wanted to get married, and write stories. It was while he was unemployed and homeless that he started to accomplish both of those dreams. He began writing badly written novels and since then learned how incredibly terrible he is at it.

Thankfully he persisted and uses his podcast, Between Lewis & Lovecraft as well as his serial shorts as a way to grow. All the while learning to be a better man for his wife and newborn son. He pretends to live in the Pacific Northwest but really lives between pages of his favorite books.

You can follow his adventures and get updates on The Penny Lich by signing up for his newsletter through his website;
TWClawson.com

Lightning Source UK Ltd.
Milton Keynes UK
UKHW020932310123
416239UK00017B/817